To Greg
from David, Denise & Sandy
Christmas 1990

THE DAYS CANADA STOOD STILL

THE DAYS CANADA STOOD STILL

Canada vs USSR 1972

Scott Morrison

Introduction by
R. Alan Eagleson

McGRAW-HILL RYERSON LIMITED
Toronto   Montreal

Canadian Cataloguing in Publication Data

Morrison, Scott
   The Days Canada Stood Still
   Canada vs USSR 1972

ISBN 0-07-549776-X

1. Canada-U.S.S.R. Hockey Series, 1972.*
I. Title.

GV847.7.M67 1989   796.96'2   C89-094390-7

Art Direction: Steven Baine/Design UYA Inc.
Production Co-ordination: W M Enterprises
Photographs: Melchior DiGiacomo/Bruce Bennett Studios

PRODUCED BY KAMIN & HOWELL INC.
for McGraw-Hill Ryerson Limited

DEDICATION

To all of Team Canada 1972, for the memories. And to my mother and father for all the right reasons, but also for letting me stay home from school on September 28, 1972.

CONTENTS

ACKNOWLEDGMENTS

A sincere word of thanks to Pat Grier, a bright, young journalist with the *Toronto Sun*, whose assistance with research and interviews was invaluable, although we did succeed in fixing a price for his services.

Thanks also to Alan Eagleson, the entire entourage, journalist Dick Beddoes, and of course, all the Team Canada players, for their time, insights and interest in this project, but mostly for the thrills they gave the hockey world in 1972.

Introduction

The 1972 Canada/Soviet Series is *the* outstanding sports event in Canada's history. All Canadians over six years of age in 1972 remember to this day where they were and what they were doing on September 28, 1972, when Paul Henderson scored The Goal.

The first days of planning for the series took place in the late sixties. Hockey Canada was formed to create an opportunity for Canada's best players to play against any other country's best players. The late Charlie Hay, Chairman of Hockey Canada, worked with this goal in mind and sought the help of the NHL Players' Association and the National Hockey League.

In 1969, I travelled to Stockholm for the world championships. With the assistance of Gordon Juckes of the Canadian Amateur Hockey Association, and Aggie Kukulowicz of Air Canada as my interpreter, I met with representatives of all major hockey countries. I told them what our best players wanted to achieve under the direction of Hockey Canada.

In the spring of 1972, at the world championships in Prague, representatives of Hockey Canada, the C.A.H.A. and the Government of Canada finalized the details with the Soviet representatives. The eight-game series with the Soviets, two games with the Swedes, and one game with the Czechoslovakians were arranged as part of Hockey Canada's goals in international hockey.

From April through August, negotiations took place with the other countries and with the National Hockey League. But in April the late Clarence Campbell, President of the NHL, stated that no NHL player would be permitted to play for Canada.

Then the NHL Players' Association obtained assurances from the top players in the league that they would honour the commitment I had made on their behalf to Hockey Canada and to the Soviet Union, Czechoslovakia and Sweden.

The emergence of the World Hockey Association created another obstacle to the series. We were obliged to drop five players from our Team Canada roster, including Bobby Hull, because of the NHL-WHA legal dispute. As Red Fisher then of the *Montreal Star* said, "it was a roller-coaster series of emotions. A team of All-Stars became an 'All Star Team.'"

The memories of the series will stay with me and all Canadian sports fans forever. The heroics of Phil Esposito and Paul Henderson and the contributions from all the other players and management have survived the passage of time.

Our team was made up of a cross-section of the Canadian ethnic mosaic. Team Canada was composed of players who were French Canadian, Ukrainian Canadians, Polish Canadians, German Canadians, Italian Canadians and other first-generation Canadians. We also had representatives of third- and fourth-generation Canadians. The mixture of backgrounds was an important ingredient in the success of our team.

It was the ultimate hockey series of our time. I am proud to have played a part in its creation, and as a Canadian who is fiercely nationalistic, I am prouder still of the way in which we won the series. We came from behind on their ice, with their rules, and in their country.

Go, Canada, go!

R. ALAN EAGLESON, Q.C.
Executive Director
National Hockey League Players' Association

CHAPTER ONE

"Henderson has scored for Canada..."

"**C**ournoyer has it on that wing. Here's a shot. Henderson makes a wild stab for it and falls. Here's another shot. Right in front. They score! Henderson has scored for Canada..."

It perhaps wasn't the most memorable description of a goal ever provided by the late Foster Hewitt, the man who first gave the world, "He shoots, He scores." But it really didn't matter. The picture spoke volumes then; the memories speak volumes now.

"I was out west recently and this couple were telling me about how they had split up in 1972 and decided to get a divorce," recalled Paul Henderson. "Well, the husband came back to the house one day to pick up a few things and say his good-byes, and the final game was on the television.

"So the two of them sat down and watched the third period,

and when I scored that goal, they both jumped up, started yelling they looked at each other and they realized that they still loved each other.

"In their letter, they wrote: 'You not only saved our country, but you saved our marriage, too.' Yes, it certainly was an amazing series. Unforgettable."

"Henderson has scored for Canada..."

They are a quintet of words that concluded a passionate roller-coaster ride of emotions for seemingly an entire nation seventeen years ago...a heady odyssey from supreme shock, to overwhelming doubt, to unbridled joy, to sheer relief, before more utter joy. The twenty-seven days Canada stood still.

The date was September 28, 1972, a day and a hockey game that refuses to quit the memory of a country that has, strangely enough, pressed to its heart only precious few moments from its polite past. But hockey has not only been a passion, but almost a religion, a metaphor for Canadian life.

And the mere mention of that goal prompts a mad flood of memories, from those who were involved, to the die-hard fans, to just plain good ol' Canadian folk. It has become a piece of Canadiana that will not fade or falter, either, because of its special oneness, the indelible place it has found in our history, and the brilliance and staggering dramatics of the series in which it was scored.

"When I came back, people were saying to me, 'Well, you just wrote yourself into the Canadian history books,'" continued Henderson. "And I would say to them, 'Get serious.' But as time goes on, seventeen years later, it becomes more and more evident I did."

"Henderson has scored for Canada…"

The occasion was the first-ever summit series, 1972, eight games between Team Canada and the Soviet Union, the first time our best professional hockey players played their best so-called amateurs. It was a series that would at long last solve the question of international hockey supremacy, a series that would answer our demand to finally allow our best to meet theirs. It was team versus team, and country versus country, the ultimate showdown.

"It was our society against theirs, and as far as we were concerned it was a damn war," said Team Canada centre Phil Esposito, still somewhat less than enamoured by the Soviet people, their system, their country, and in large part even the concept of the series itself, although ultimately there was no other place he would have rather been.

"I had to play," he adds, stopping short of providing an explanation that was not really necessary. It was hockey, it had become a matter of national pride, and it was history. The best players simply had to be there because the country was calling.

"Don't ever think otherwise about that series, though," continued Esposito. "It was war and it was hell. Man oh man, it was something else."

But it was also all so very special, perhaps more than for just the fact that it was the first, and the assembled talent was so damn good, but for how the series unfolded, its unpredictability, its many upsets and comebacks, and because the compelling issue was not settled until there were just thirty-four seconds remaining in the final game.

"Henderson has scored for Canada…"

"It was a great series because both teams played so well," said Team Canada winger Ron Ellis. "If it had been a cakewalk, which a lot of people expected, and we had blown them away, no one would even remember the series today. But because it was so close, well, that's what made it special, unforgettable.

"Hey, this thing was country versus country, our beliefs and values against another set of beliefs and values. There's no question if they beat us they were going to use it to their advantage, to tell the world they were the best. This was more than just a hockey series, whether it was the first or not."

With Paul Henderson's goal at 19:26 of the third period of the eighth game, Team Canada rallied to win this historic summit, which had become almost a lesson in humility. It was a series they were supposed to have swept, but wound up winning by only a narrow 4-3-1 margin, miraculously winning the final three games in the Luzhniki Arena in Moscow.

With that stunning final game, a 6-5 victory, Canada had saved face and could proudly stick out its collective chest and declare itself the number-one hockey nation in the world. But out of that series also came a stark new realization and appreciation for the Soviet game, and in return one for ours. They were supposed to expose the mediocrity of the Soviet system, but instead learned more about themselves. The discoveries were an unexpected charm.

"It was like a Hollywood script — the whole series was like that," said Canadian centre Peter Mahovlich. "We all thought it would be a significant series, for the development of hockey and all that, but I don't think any of us knew how far reaching it would be. I mean, this series dramatically changed the whole world of hockey. And it changed a few people along the way, too.

"In Canada, we relate so much to hockey. It's a part of our heritage. This was one of those few moments in our history that was, well, a rallying cry. People with different views, people with different politics, different religions, all came together as one, for one very special moment. Something like that doesn't happen very often."

It hasn't happened since, either. There have been exciting series and thrilling games, but nothing of the proportions of that first series, which dripped with drama and intrigue and, before it was over, transcended the boundaries of sport.

"During that series," said Henderson, "there was no such thing as a Francophone or a Westerner, or anything else. We were all Canadians. The series brought all Canadians together. It brought an entire country together. It was Canada playing, not Team Canada. It was us against them and every Canadian somehow seemed to have a sense of ownership of that team. I guess war is the only other thing that could bring a country together like that series did."

And it was a war, of sorts. An ideological war that was fought through eight memorable games on a hockey rink, using rubber bullets, the issue in the beginning being simply hockey superiority, but ultimately becoming a conflict of cultures and beliefs and systems.

"We just thought it would be another hockey series," offered winger Frank Mahovlich. "We had no real idea of the scope and of how it would be remembered. But it didn't take very long before we knew we were into something big. Really big."

It was a series that would also have a profound influence on the hockey world, financially and sociologically. It drew apart the Iron Curtain and opened up borders for exchanges never previously contemplated, and it continues to be remembered in the two countries, though understandably with a decidedly different reverence.

"The series became part of our national heritage," said Team Canada coach Harry Sinden. "There's no doubt about the measure of posterity it gained. Maybe it's because what happened wasn't anticipated. Maybe it's because it was fantastic hockey... and we won.

"Maybe it's all of those things. But it's something none of us involved in it will ever forget. You see the players today and there's a common bond there. We were a unique team, the first one ever put together for a series of that kind. It's like I told the players, winning the Stanley Cup is very special, but a lot of people have their names on the Stanley Cup. We're the only ones who have won an eight-game series with the Soviets."

Even to the usually staid Soviets, who were numbed by what had evolved into a shocking defeat, deep down the series remains special, though certainly not the fondest memory they might own. To the oldtimers, the veterans of the 1972 summit, it will never be forgotten.

"The first series will always be the most special," said former Soviet centre Boris Mikhailov, whose name over those eight games became as well known as, perhaps, even that of Henderson. Mikhailov is now an assistant coach with the famed Central Red Army team and a frequent visitor to North America for hockey tours.

"We didn't know a lot about the pros from the NHL and they had only a very slight knowledge about us. But for the world of hockey, it was an historical event. It opened the windows of the world.

"It was a meeting between two schools of hockey and we have since continued this great exchange and we have learned from each other, taking the best of both styles. That's the most important result of the series now, that we were able to learn and continue to meet each other. It has meant a lot for the game of hockey. I was very happy just to have the chance to meet the NHL superstars. They did not only have a good team, but good guys. That is something you don't forget.

"I really thought — I suppose we all thought this way and maybe that was our ultimate downfall — that we had the series won when we returned home ahead. I will always be very bitter about what happened in that series in the end. But still, I also have very special memories of that series. I will always have them."

It's a series that for countless years seemed as though it would remain only a distant dream of its organizers, never to overcome the politics of international hockey, the firm and divergent views of the Canadian and European hockey officials, specifically the hierarchy of the International Ice Hockey Federation (IIHF), governing body of all the world tournaments. Professionals, paid players, were simply not permitted to compete internationally, and only in recent years have they been given access to the Olympic hockey tournament. Beyond that, it was the Soviets with whom the agreement for the summit ultimately had to be struck, a difficult and always frustrating task.

But a compilation of major events in the late 1960s, which included Canada's withdrawal from international competition in 1970, soon changed the thinking of the hockey powers, and soon the face of the game.

The beginning was February, 1969, after a fourth-place showing at the world championships, with the formation of a body known as Hockey Canada, which was born of a government task force ordered a year earlier by then Prime Minister Pierre Elliott Trudeau and created by Health and Welfare Minister John Munro. Within a four-year period the summit series was reality.

It was the objective of Hockey Canada, which was given jurisdiction over the country's international hockey endeavours, to pursue "open competition" — meaning the use of professional hockey players — as well as the super series.

"I remember back in 1968," recalled Alan Eagleson, then a board member with Hockey Canada and now its chief international negotiator, and also executive director of the National Hockey League Players' Association. "I started with Hockey Canada then, and the chairman at the time, Charlie Hay, had the idea of our best playing against the Soviets' best. Then it all started to come together in 1969 in Stockholm at the world championships."

It was there that the national team finished fourth in the six-team round robin, winning just four of ten games. They were sadly out-matched and it was evident that the best talent Canada could assemble would never make waves on the international pond unless rules were changed, unless at the very least the Soviets would agree to meet at the summit.

At the IIHF annual congress in July at Lausanne, Switzerland, Hockey Canada proposed allowing for a team of professionals and amateurs to compete the following year in the world championship, the games scheduled to be played in Montreal and Winnipeg.

That motion was unanimously rejected by the IIHF. However, another was tabled, one allowing for the use of nine former professionals. That vote ended in a tie, but was pushed through by IIHF president J.F. "Bunny" Ahearne for a one-year trial. At those same meetings, the 1970 world championships were taken away from Canada, which prompted Canada's decision to pull out of international hockey. A year later, they withdrew from the 1972 Olympic Games.

"I met with all the organizers (in the IIHF) and there was talk about having the NHL all-stars meeting the Russians in a series," continued Eagleson. "I set up a meeting the next day at 9 a.m. with the Soviets, but they were playing some games. They said they couldn't talk to me because I wasn't with the CAHA (Canadian Amateur Hockey Association).

"So I set up a meeting for 1 p.m. and I told them I would bring along Gordon Juckes, who was the executive director of the CAHA. Then they said they had to talk to Clarence Campbell, who was president of the NHL at the time.

"Then I got smart. I had a telex sent from the ambassador saying, 'Please advise the Soviets that I would like to meet with the Soviets in Sweden or in Moscow and advise them that I (Eagleson) am the lawyer for the workers, the guys who are going to play in this series.' Within two hours we had our meeting. On April 8, I met again with Andrei Starovoitov, who was the chief Soviet delegate and my counterpart. It all started coming together in 1969."

In April, 1972, at the world championship in Prague, Czechoslovakia, the breakthrough was finally made. The negotiating team of Hay, CAHA president Joe Kryczka, and, Lou Lefaive reached an agreement with the Soviet delegation for an eight-game series to be played the following September, with the first four games to be played in Canada, the final four in Moscow.

"I remember when it finally broke in 1972," continued Eagleson. "Doug Fisher and Charlie Hay were at the world championships and I remember getting a rush call to come over and sit down and finalize the plans for an eight-game deal. We knew this was something special then, but not even we could visualize what would come out of all this.

"We made an $800,000 profit from that series — that was it. I thought it was the start of something interesting, but I never thought it would become the business that it has over the years. International hockey has put in excess of $25-million of new money into hockey, money that wouldn't have been there otherwise.

"It has been very important for the players' pension plan, but it has also had its rewards for the fans. It opened up the hockey world and we've seen some outstanding hockey as a result."

Eagleson's involvement in the negotiations and later the preparations grew because of his role as the players' union chief. He could guarantee the talent. Even when the late Clarence Campbell, president of the NHL, declared his players would not be allowed to play, Eagleson corrected him by stating his clients would. And, while wearing his other hat of player agent, he had a solid majority of the premier players in his stable.

Predictably there were logistical headaches in organizing the series, beginning with dealing with the sometimes indecisive Soviets and arranging for travel for two teams and their entourages, as well as securing a lucrative television package and selling promotional rights. Toward that end, Eagleson sold the advertising rights to a group that included Bobby Orr and Harold Ballard for $750,000. The return was in excess of $1-million.

There was also the need to assure NHL owners, particularly those in the American centres, they should not be overly concerned about having their top stars, despite the risk of injury, play for Team Canada. William Jennings, of the New York Rangers, and Weston Adams, of the Boston Bruins, were probably the most outspoken opponents, the latter at first declaring he would not allow Esposito or Orr to participate.

The owners' reservations were quickly assuaged, however, after Eagleson's confirmation that the series would profit the players' pension fund, money the owners would otherwise have had to ante up themselves. Fiscal responsibility can put to rest many fears and has continued to do so seventeen years later. Hockey Canada also arranged for additional insurance, which eased some of the doubts the players shared.

But there were other concerns, notably over the ground rules, particularly the use of amateur officials for the games in Canada, and the use of European officials for the games in Moscow. The timing of the series wasn't great, either. And the players weren't being paid; they were given only modest expenses for themselves and their wives.

At the time, too, the rival World Hockey Association happened on the scene, and was beginning to revolutionize the game from a financial standpoint, offering huge salaries to NHL stars.

Among them, and at the time the most notable signing, was Chicago Blackhawks' superstar left winger Bobby Hull, who took the lure of $2-million from the Winnipeg Jets. Afterwards, the likes of Derek Sanderson, J.C. Tremblay and Gerry Cheevers would follow.

While Hull was named on the original thirty-five-man roster of Team Canada, and coach Harry Sinden had at first promised he would play, the agreement clearly stipulated Hull would not. Only players signed to NHL contracts by August 13, the day before the opening of Team Canada's training camp, were being allowed to represent their country.

This was, after all, a partnership of the NHL and Hockey Canada, and it meant WHA players weren't welcome. Predictably there was soon a huge public outcry, with support mounting across the country for Hull to be allowed to play. Even Prime Minister Trudeau was eventually asked to intervene, and "To Russia with Hull" became the rallying cry of the masses. Alas, "To Hull with Russia" was the final plaintive sigh, Hull not allowed to play until two years later when the WHA assembled its own Team Canada.

"It was the most disappointing time of my career," said Hull. "And the people who were responsible were Eagleson and Campbell. It wasn't a Canadian team, it was Team NHL. It sure as hell wasn't Canadian. I'm not saying I would've made the team, but they wouldn't give me the chance. From the time the season ended, I was involved in negotiations with the WHA. I never talked to anyone with Team Canada...Team NHL."

Curiously, while still an NHL employee, eligible to play and expected to do so, in the spring of 1972, during the Stanley Cup playoffs, Hull voiced concerns about the series that would become prophetic a few months later. Later still they would become the most often heard criticisms of these international ventures for the decade to follow.

"Such a series should be played under our rules, in mid-season or after the NHL season when we are in top condition," said Hull back then. "There is no way we would be in top physical shape to play them eight games in September, and those Russians are never out of shape. They would be working constantly at hockey when we would be engaged in our regular off-season occupations. Don't forget, this is a series in which we have everything to lose and very little to gain."

Seventeen years later, Hull said, "I knew if the Soviet Union was about to challenge the NHL, they must've thought they could win. They had been building and building for that moment. That's the one thing I did know."

It's a sentiment that was echoed by Esposito seventeen years later and a reasonable excuse-in-waiting when it appeared the Canadians were doomed at the summit.

"We trained for two weeks for that series," said Esposito. "It was August 14 when we reported to training camp in Toronto. I remember that day because it was my daughter's birthday. I had a hockey school going then, too. Everything was booked a long time before that series came along, but we had to give back a whole bunch of money to the kids at the school. A lot of us had to give up a lot of things to play in that series."

"Phil didn't want to go," said brother Tony Esposito. "I didn't really want to get involved in that summer stuff, either, the baloney of it all, the politics. That stuff. But we felt we had to go."

Bobby Clarke said, "You kidding? There's no way I could've turned down the invite. You just had to be there as a player."

As the brother of the famed Golden Jet, Dennis Hull could have been excused for saying *nyet* to the offer, but after consultation with his older brother, he determined it was an experience they both should not miss, although a certain bitterness remained.

"They were a far more talented team than we were," remembered Dennis Hull of the Soviets, adding, "but then there were a lot of guys who should have played for us and didn't because of the WHA.

"I wasn't going to go because of Bobby not being there, but Bobby talked to me and said I should I go. I'm glad he did. But I also realize, had he been invited, I wouldn't have been invited. The NHL was just trying to show how fair it could be by asking me to go along."

Another scratch, but innocent enough because of injury, was Bruins' star defenceman Bobby Orr, who would have his career frequently interrupted and ultimately prematurely concluded because of chronic knee ailments. Despite his injury, he owned a faint hope he might overcome it and be able to play, and so remained and travelled with the team throughout the series. Even if unable to play, he realized something big was in the works.

"To me, ours was one of the great teams in the history of sport, and that was one of the greatest series ever," said Orr. "It was a war. It was unbelievable. There'll never be another series like it, either. You can have all the Canada Cups you want, and they've been wonderful, but this was the first and the best.

"What that team did, well, it was just one helluva team. I remember it like it was yesterday."

Despite the outcome, and the accolades bestowed on the series, there are some, such as Esposito, though brilliant throughout, a leader, and arguably Team Canada's most valuable player, who always had doubts, reservations and complaints, particularly about playing in the Soviet Union.

"It wasn't great over there," said Esposito. "It was lousy. It was especially terrible for me. I hated it. The place scared me. I thought they would kill to win and that scared me."

Added brother Tony, "It was a great series, no question, but it was sure a helluva lot better when it was over."

Still, to many of the players, the series, while exacting a huge emotional and physical toll, became something of a blessing both in their lives and careers. When it was over, they had become living legends, demigods. They had shaped history, their exploits never to be forgotten. Even to Phil Esposito it was the turning point in a career that was already a huge success, but strangely devoid of the proper recognition it deserved.

"People were always underestimating me," he said wryly. "Then I had to go ruin it all over there with a good series and make everyone take notice. Damn."

"I know I never knew what the series was about when I got asked to training camp," admitted Bruins' defenceman Don Awrey, a solid, if unspectacular player, who has a wonderful self-deprecating sense of humour. "I knew when it was announced that I wasn't one of the eight or ten best defencemen in the National Hockey League, so I never figured on going.

"But then Orr was injured, and a few of the other guys couldn't go, so they kept going down the list until they got to me. So even before they had asked me I said yes.

"I don't think anyone expected the series to have the intensity it did. Everyone figured they would all get a chance to play, but the way it worked out, well, they had to go with their best guys to win it."

A laugher, as they say in the lexicon of sport, is what the series was supposed to have been, an eight-game romp for the Canadians, erasing once and for all any doubts that might have existed as to which country was hockey's real superpower. It was, of course, anything but a laugher.

It began on a steamy night in Montreal, with a shocking 7-3 loss to the Soviets after the Canadians had scored twice in the first seven minutes. It continued two nights later in Toronto, with the Canadians rallying to win 4-1, a tough game that gave them an indication of how truly difficult the series would become. And no one was laughing.

In game three in Winnipeg, as they continued the tour across the country, Team Canada allowed a lead to slip away, and was actually quite fortunate to escape with a 4-4 tie. Next stop was Vancouver, the absolute low point in the series, where they were humiliated 5-3, outplayed by the comrades and put off by the Canadian fans, who had showered them with verbal abuse throughout.

The country was right behind Team Canada then — win or tie. That prompted an emotional, heartfelt speech by Phil Esposito on national television following the game, a plea for support and a scolding for lack thereof. It was a speech that ultimately banded together a confused, struggling hockey team.

From there it was off to Sweden for a series of exhibition games, a time when the team finally began drawing together, working itself into shape, developing a cohesion on and off the ice. Oddly enough, even as they came together they grew apart; three disgruntled players left after they arrived in Moscow, with a fourth to follow.

The order confronting them was obviously tall, and it seemed to grow a lot taller after the fifth game in Moscow, when another lead was surrendered and the Soviets won 5-4, pressing the Canadians' backs firmly to the wall. They needed to win the final three games to capture the series and salvage their pride.

It was then, in game six, that Henderson assumed his hero's status, scoring the winner in a 3-2 nail-biter of a victory. Henderson provided the winning goal two days later, too, this a 4-3 triumph. Then along came game eight and the rest, as they say, is glorious history.

Ken Dryden said, "It became an awful lot of different things — that was part of it. It was more cultural than anything else. It was a series that in the end came to attract all that attention. There was a sense of it being our team at the start, nobody's team for a while, then our team at the end. Actually, I think the attachment was always there. It was just the anger and the emotion when things were turning out as expected.

"What made it such a vivid experience is that we went from being as low as we were to as high as we went in such a short period of time. Let me correct that — within a fairly extended period of time. When you live through it, there were many days to feel down and some days to feel the ups. It wasn't like the middle of game when you score a couple of goals to come back, but there's no time to really experience it. We had time in this series to feel everything, and that's what gave it an added dimension.

We went from the utter disappointment of the opening game to the improbable ending, from one end to the other, in the same series."

"I don't know if we as Canadians have had a greater adventure," commented writer/broadcaster Dick Beddoes, who covered the series for the *Globe and Mail.* "It was the greatest adventure this country has ever seen. Fifteen million people, at the time two-thirds of the population, were either tuned into radio or watching on television. We've never had that sort of feeling. If you went to Hollywood and gave them the script, they'd say you were filled to the gills with cocaine or something. There's no way it would work, but it did. And there were a lot of marvellously coincidental things that happened."

"It was a hard, tough series," said Canadian winger Yvon Cournoyer, who assisted on the memorable winning goal in the final game. "I talked to some Russians two years ago at an oldtimers' game, and they were saying that for them it was still the biggest series ever.

"It was for us, too. It's something that, seventeen years later, people are still talking about. They can still remember where they were when the series was on, when Paul scored that winning goal. It's a once-in-a-lifetime thing. I remember where I was when President Kennedy got shot. This series is like that, a big event that touched a lot of people."

One man who wasn't surprised by the startling turn the series took, that it was closer and more dramatic than almost anyone had anticipated, was former Toronto Maple Leaf winger Billy Harris, who in 1969 had his amateur status reinstated and played for the Canadian national team. Two years later, he coached the Swedish national team, and later still Team Canada WHA in the 1974 summit.

"I called the Soviets to win the series 4-3-1," said Harris, his prediction almost as much an indictment of the Canadian's over-confidence and inadequate preparation as the Soviets' under-estimated skills. "With ten minutes to go, the Soviets leading 5-3 in that final game, I had a pretty good feeling about that prediction, too.

"The reason is that I had played against them when I got reinstated in the national team in 1969. We played them in the Izvestia tournament and I had coached against them in 1971-72. So over two years, I had seen quite a bit of the Soviets as a player and as a coach. Everyone else seemed to think the Soviets would be humiliated, but I knew it wouldn't happen, and that's how I made my prediction.

"I remember one day before the series started, telling the Soviet coaching staff, through an interpreter, to relax, that they weren't going to embarrass themselves. A lot of people had predicted 12-0 games, wipeouts, and after the first couple of minutes in Montreal, when Team Canada was ahead 2-0, that's how it looked. I was going to slip out of the Forum.

"I'm sure, though, that the players on Team Canada went through the same experience I went through in 1969 when I played the Soviets for the first time. You just figure because you're an NHL player you can go end to end ten or eleven times and score six or seven goals.

"We were led to believe we were so far superior, but when I was playing, I got the crap kicked out of me by the Soviets and the Czechoslovakians. They were tough, physical players with a lot of skill. I knew it was going to be a close series, and it wasn't until the Canadians began showing some respect for their opposition that they got back into it. And that they were able to get back in it and win three games over there, well, it's amazing what they were able to do."

It mightn't have been quite how Charlie Hay had envisioned it back in 1968, then again it might have been better, for this was a series that not only introduced the Soviets to the North American fans and players and opened everyone's eyes to a different way to prepare and play the game, but it quite nicely highlighted qualities for which Canadian teams have since become famous: grit, heart and determination. On the ice, you can match a team with skill, as the Russians obviously were able to do, but they lacked the same emotion, a sometimes decisive intangible.

"The series is a great memory," said defenceman Brad Park. "It does have a great place in our history. I think it would whether we won or not. But it's just the way it worked out. It was like a Walt Disney movie."

Most remarkable, though, is how the series tugged the heart of a country, at first upsetting it, then mesmerizing it, stealing its attention and, eventually, its support. Throughout the country on the day Henderson made history, schools and businesses ground to a halt as the final game progressed. A nation was taken hostage by its emotions and its heritage.

"The series was the greatest thing for our generation," said Eagleson. "There are three things that, as Canadians, stand out for us, that we remember where we were when: President Kennedy was shot; the first man walked on the moon; and Paul Henderson scored the winning goal in the 1972 series.

"When (sprinter) Ben Johnson won that race in the Summer Olympics, I saw a euphoria I hadn't seen in Canada since the Henderson goal. But that feeling soon disappeared, it faded fast, but the Henderson goal lives on forever.

"You have to remember, it was a series of democracy versus communism, no question, and we used everything along those lines to try and stir things up. It was the most important sporting event ever in Canada. The excitement has never been matched and it has never really died."

And that is, indeed, the truest measure of an event's significance and impact, of how it stands the passing of time. In those terms, this series has lost precious little, and if anything, its memory has only been rekindled by the subsequent series it has spawned, most recent of course the outstanding three-game Canada Cup final between Team Canada and the Soviets. Ironically, the final game of that series, on September 15, 1987, ended 6-5, with Mario Lemieux scoring with 1:26 remaining in the third period. At the end of the rink, Lemieux stood pressed against the boards, his arms high in the air in celebration, embraced by his teammates. It was almost the very same picture of Paul Henderson in 1972.

"That series (1972) will always be the greatest," said Eagleson. "But what the 1987 Canada Cup did was solve a generation gap for us. It was getting to the point the past few years where I was talking to high-school classes and the kids had no knowledge of the 1972 series because they were simply too young. They had heard of it, they knew we won, they knew Henderson scored the winning goal, but they hadn't seen the series and really didn't know how great it was.

"But then along comes the Wayne Gretzky-Mario Lemieux combo in 1987 — they put on a great show in the three-game final with the Soviets — bring back memories of '72 for a lot of us, and produce the second most exciting series ever, but also one the kids of today saw and will remember. It bridged a generation gap, but the first one is still the best one."

"The '72 series became a piece of Canadian culture," said Ellis. "It's unfortunate we weren't here to see the effects it had on the Canadian people, of how they all pulled together. In that sense, we really didn't feel the effect of it.

"But it's a piece of history those who played in the series or just watched it will never forget. They'll pass it on to their grandchildren. You can't imagine how special it is to be involved in a series like that, the first, and a series that will be remembered for a long, long time."

Perhaps touched most by it, though, was Henderson, whose career assumed a grand new prominence, and whose life was drastically changed.

"It was the thrill of a lifetime," said Henderson, a competent NHL winger prior to the series, a national hero afterwards. "As soon as it was over, well, it was like war. Those last four games, I vowed to myself to never get that emotionally involved in anything again, and I haven't.

"It's nice to reminisce about the series. I can't think of a better thing to be associated with and remembered for. The stories I hear, and I keep getting them even today from people across the country, it's just amazing how that one hockey series touched so many people's lives, and not just ours.

"I bet that I talk about the goals I scored 300 days a year

now, and as it gets further away, I seem to talk about them more and more. And I find myself saying, 'Goodness gracious, did I really do that? Did that really happen?' But you know what? On the replays I still haven't missed yet."

"Henderson has scored for Canada…"

"The game is over and Canada has won the series," is how Foster Hewitt ended that historical broadcast. "It was a thrilling, hard-fought tussle, and it showed the quality of the Canadian team, able to win three of four games on Moscow ice.

"They came back and redeemed themselves after a slow start in Canada. They weren't in shape, but they got better and better and they fought like tigers."

Seventeen years later, this is their story, through the eyes of the tigers — the players, the coaches and the organizers of Team Canada, or Team 50 (the number in the official travelling party), as they called themselves.

CHAPTER TWO

Opening Night

"From the beginning it was like a reunion for all the National Hockey League players — just make sure you have enough film for the camera," recalled Billy Harris, the former NHL player and coach, who had predicted a Soviet victory in the series. "They sure didn't seem too concerned, that's for sure. But then, they didn't know any better, either."

It was on August 14, 1972, almost a full month before the National Hockey League training camps were scheduled to open, that Team Canada first assembled in Toronto at Maple Leaf Gardens to begin preparations for the landmark eight-game summit series against the Soviet Union.

Thirty-five players, with only a handful of exceptions essentially the best in professional hockey, all working for just expense money, all surrendering their already short summers, promised to play. They all expected to romp over the hated comrades, the so-called gifted amateurs.

It was a time, too, when players did not spend a lot of time in the summer concerning themselves with fitness. A few weeks before training camp they would begin light workouts, play their way into shape through the exhibition season, and be in high gear after the first thirty or so games. A practice that would drastically change after the series, of course, it was almost the undoing of Team Canada in 1972.

It was in part why they owned just a slight sense of apprehension, but the main reason for apprehension was that the quality of the opposition wasn't fully known. Or appreciated. There were never any real self-doubts, at least not until the series began. Any lingering misgivings that might have existed during training camp were overcome by the confidence fortified by the nineteen days of practice, during which the now infamous scouting report compiled by Bob Davidson and the late Johnny McLellan was delivered, and every time they turned on a television, opened a newspaper, or listened to fans.

The Soviets had dominated international hockey because Canada was not represented by its best — that was the popular sentiment. That domination, Canadians insisted, would mercilessly end, and Canada would be restored to the prominence it had not enjoyed since the 1950s.

"It was a party, one big happy time," explained winger Dennis Hull. "You're with all these new friends and you're the centre of attention. We thought it was great. This was the first time a team like this had been put together, and here we are with all these guys we knew and had been playing against."

"I have lots of fond memories of that time," said winger Rod Gilbert. "I was going through an emotional period then. I'd been with the New York Rangers for about ten years, and I had seen the team go from last to first that year. It was just around all the World Hockey Association stuff.

"I was negotiating my contract with the Rangers and they had offered me about $90,000. Then the Cleveland team with the WHA, offers $300,000. It was pretty difficult to decide. I knew, too, that if I had jumped to the WHA, I would've missed the series. So when I went to Toronto for training camp I had Jean Ratelle with me. He was still negotiating.

"I still hadn't signed and I was worried about that, but then the Rangers offered to increase my salary, so when I did sign, well, that was very pleasing for me. I had a new contract and I was staying with the Rangers, so when I got to training camp I was on a high already.

"It wasn't the greatest setup, though. The training camp was really disorganized, because we didn't know what we were up against. All the scouting reports were negative about the Russians — I mean, no one had really seen them play. And the players, well, we were cutting our vacations short, trying to get back into shape, and there was no guarantee of money. But despite all that, everyone was into it. We were proud of having been selected to play for our country.

"But the intensity just wasn't there in training camp. We felt we were so much superior, and that's what everyone kept telling us, too — the scouts, the media. So the training camp really wasn't what it should have been. Plus, you've got thirty-five players, guys who were the best players on their teams, and no one knows who's going to play. So everything was pretty uncertain."

It was every fear head coach Harry Sinden had anticipated, actually, and perhaps more. Entering the training camp, knowing the egos with which he had to deal, the dissatisfaction of being in training in summer, of not being paid…Sinden was never quite sure how to handle his team of stars, or how they would react to him. But he soon found out.

"I was aware of what might happen, but the problem was I couldn't convince the players of what might happen," said Sinden, who in 1970 had coached the Boston Bruins to their first Stanley Cup in twenty-nine years, but resigned to enter private business when denied a modest raise. Ironically, his company went bankrupt just prior to his being asked to coach and manage the team.

Sinden was the obvious choice, too, out of work and with international experience, having played for the Kitchener-Waterloo Dutchmen in the 1960 Olympic Games and captained the Whitby Dunlops to a world championship victory over the Soviets in 1958 in Oslo, Norway.

"I knew the Russians pretty well, and I knew they were strong enough to give us a tough game," said Sinden. "I just didn't think they'd beat us the way they did. I tried to tell the players, but they didn't listen. After that first game, though, when I talked, they listened."

It was obvious from the beginning that Team Canada had sufficient talent to win, having the two top goalies in the game; a solid, mobile defence, and fourteen of the top twenty-five scorers in the NHL the previous season. Defensively they would be strong, and firepower would not be a problem, not with the likes of Phil Esposito, who had scored a record seventy-six goals the previous season, and Vic Hadfield (fifty goals), Yvon Cournoyer (forty-seven), Ratelle (forty-six), Gilbert and Frank Mahovlich (forty-three). They had size, they had speed, and they had character, the depth of which they could never have envisioned.

"Harry and I agreed on almost every player that came to camp," said assistant coach John Ferguson. "Only in July did Harry and I go our separate ways. We differed on two players, Walt Tkzacuk, who made it easy by saying he wouldn't be available, and Don Awrey, who eventually played. Harry wanted him, I didn't."

The problem remained conditioning and attitude, the former only upgraded later in the series, the latter immediately adjusted after opening night. That the Canadians were confident − no, overconfident − was entirely understandable. The scouting report was just so damn convincing.

The Soviets hadn't exactly been impressive at the previous world championships, or in the Winter Olympics at Sapporo, Japan, when they were tied 3-3 by the Harris-coached Swedish national team, which was mediocre at best. During those Games, a twenty-year-old goalie by the name of Vladislav Tretiak first appeared. He would attain prominence for his sheer brilliance in the summit series, but was merely very ordinary in the Olympic Games.

"I had been at the Winter Olympics in Sapporo," recalled journalist Dick Beddoes. "The Canadians had boycotted, and I saw the Soviets, but I wasn't able to transpose what I saw there to the NHL. I said before the series, the Canadians should win every period, every game."

It was also a time of transition for the Soviets, with the father of their hockey, Anatoli Tarasov, replaced as head coach of the national team by the tandem of Vsevolod Bobrov, at the time the highest scorer in Soviet history, and Boris (Chuckles) Kulagin.

In fairness to the Canadian scouting mission, they had worked under difficult, perhaps impossible, conditions on their brief tour of the Soviet Union, spending just four days there, seeing an intra-squad game, and an exhibition between the Leningrad Army squad and the Soviet Selects.

"They sent John and me to watch them work out," explained Davidson. 'But we saw just one game. It was a complete waste of time. We only saw Tretiak in one intra-squad game, and his team lost 8-1, and he gave up all the goals. We were supposed to say he was great, I guess."

What neither Davidson nor McLellan knew, however, was that Tretiak was to be married the next day. It apparently had an immense affect on his performance.

"I didn't know he was getting married the next day, either. But if we had been there for a week, it would've been fine. But we never got a chance to see anything. They had sent a couple of fellas over here to scout for a week before it was decided we should go over there. But for the time we stayed, it was a waste of money. John thought we'd win easy, take them eight straight, but I thought it would go the limit.

"The Russians didn't show us anything, but we could see they were in great shape. The problem with our guys is they figured it would be a breeze, but I told them from the start it would go to the wire. It wasn't until we treated the Soviets with a bit of respect that we started winning.

"Scouting over there, though, was a joke. We saw one game, got there just before it started, had no seats, and were cramped into the press box. You couldn't even move to get a pencil out of your pocket. We didn't have any lineups, either. We didn't know who we were looking at.

"We were criticized a lot back then for our scouting, and I still hear about it, people criticizing us. It still makes my wife mad to hear people saying things when they don't know what went on. But after watching Tretiak in that one game, I couldn't say he was good. People still bring it up periodically, but it doesn't bother me. It's like when the Rocket scored five goals in a playoff game. He's supposed to have scored them all against me. I was checking him. But he only scored three against me. And what about Babe Pratt? He was on for four of them. Oh, well, it gets your name in the papers. But I just wish we had spent two weeks in Russia. We would've come back with a lot more information."

But then, it conceivably wouldn't have been any more accurate, not with the games the Soviets play. While widely criticized for their efforts, the scouting team was simply a victim of more Soviet hijinks.

"The Russians are masters of deceit," said Bobby Hull, "but if you look at Yakushev, Tretiak, Gusev, Kharlamov and can't tell they're players, then they (the scouts) weren't much of hockey people back then. I knew what the Russians would be like. If I'd been invited to camp I could've helped get that message across."

"I remember sitting in the Forum watching the Russians practice," said reserve goalie Eddie Johnston, "and it looked like it was going to be a blowout. They screwed around, nothing went right, they just looked awful. You couldn't help but wonder about this team."

And wonder the Canadians did — for eight dramatic games.

* * *

"I can't recall any game I've ever been at feeling the tension (like this), and it keeps building up," intoned broadcaster Foster Hewitt that night, just prior to the start of the long-awaited opening game — September 2, 1972, at the Forum in Montreal.

The weeks of buildup and suspense were at last complete. A series that at one time never seemed possible was about to become reality. It was hands-across-the-waters in an international exchange, *glasnost* a decade before its time. But it was also to be serious business.

"We all were convinced we would win it eight straight. All we had to do was show up," said Alan Eagleson, head of the players' union, an organizer of the series, and chief international negotiator for Hockey Canada.

Just twenty-eight hours before the start of the series, though, there was some question whether the Soviets would indeed show. There was a minor, though potentially serious, threat of a delay, if not postponement, of proceedings, when a Montreal man obtained a court order allowing him to seize and hold the Soviets' equipment until their government produced the $1,889 in damages the court had awarded him for the demolition of his car by a Soviet tank during the 1968 Soviet invasion in Prague, Czechoslovakia.

The problem was quietly and promptly resolved. There were two stories as to how this came about. While the External Affairs office would offer no clues, one is that Prime Minister Trudeau helped to take care of business, and just to ensure proceedings started without further incident, he officiated the ceremonial face-off himself.

Another story suggests that Eagleson, who had taken charge

of the operation of the team and the series, had caught wind of the court order and handed a personal cheque to the Montreal man, then retrieved the equipment. Nothing was going to stand in the way of history. This had become Eagleson's show and the show would go on.

"The government became involved, front and centre," said Aggie Kukulowicz, a sports representative for Air Canada, who served as the interpreter for the Russians. "But when it came time to make the payments, they say, well, go ahead, Mr. Eagleson. The amount was actually $2,200 he gave the guy."

There was still one further slight scare, a haunting feeling that something might be amiss, less than two hours before the game, when the Soviets hadn't arrived at the rink. Their tardiness, however, was due to traffic congestion.

It was a hot and sweaty night in Montreal, though a script writer might ultimately have revised the description to "dark and stormy," if only he had known... There was predictable excitement, too, a capacity crowd of 18,889 squeezing into the Forum. They were here to witness a slaughter, they thought, yet there was still some uncertainty. The players felt it, too.

"We really didn't know what to expect when we stepped onto the ice," said winger Yvon Cournoyer. "We had been together nineteen days, worked hard, and we kept hearing how bad they were and how easily we would beat them. But we were all pretty nervous, that's for sure. It was the uncertainty that had everyone just a little on edge. We had been told in the scouting reports they had absolutely nothing, but we still weren't sure."

"We all just wanted to get this thing going, enough practising, let's play, that's how we felt," said defenceman Brad Park, whose wife had given birth to their first child earlier in the day. Another defenceman, Guy Lapointe, would also play the entire series despite the impending birth of his first child, then not see the child until he was eighteen days old.

Across the rink, in the Soviets' dressing room, the nerves were no less brittle, the anxiety no less acute. Despite having a more thorough knowledge of what they were up against, the Soviets weren't fully certain they were good enough to beat the Canadians. They had watched them for two days at practice, seen how well they skated, how hard they shot. It seemed they, too, had been deceived. Prior to the game, though, the late Jacques Plante, a Hall of Fame goaltender doing colour commentary on the French television network assembled for the series, visited the Soviet dressing room and, through an interpreter, alerted Tretiak to the nuances of the Canadian shooters. Plante was not a traitor; he merely feared the worst for the Soviets, didn't want them to look foolish.

"Before that first game," said Soviet centre Boris Mikhailov, "we had a very nervous feeling. It was scary. We just wanted to begin playing."

And so the first chapter in an historic series began.

"I thought we conducted a good training camp," said Ferguson. "All the players had mutually agreed to play, so there wasn't any problem getting them to work. We were looking at the cream of the crop in the NHL. Yeah, the scouting was a problem, but you couldn't really get a good look at that team. The scouts only saw them in one game, and there was no videotape then. It was all done using the reels — pretty primitive. But we thought we were ready."

Sinden chose to start Ken Dryden in goal, the lanky goalie for the hometown Montreal Canadiens, who also had experience at the international level. He would be backed up by Chicago Blackhawks' Tony Esposito.

Allowed to dress just seventeen skaters, Sinden decided to use only five defencemen: Rangers' Rod Seiling and Brad Park, Detroit Red Wings' veteran Gary Bergman, Bruins' Don Awrey, and Lapointe, also of the Canadiens.

Up front, Bruins' sharpshooter Phil Esposito centred Canadiens' wingers Frank Mahovlich and Yvon Cournoyer, while the Rangers' GAG (Goal a Game) line of Gilbert, Ratelle and Hadfield remained intact. The third line consisted of Philadelphia Flyers' young centre Bobby Clarke, flanked by a pair of Toronto Maple Leafs, Paul Henderson and Ron Ellis, with the fourth line comprised of Canadiens' centre Peter Mahovlich, St. Louis Blues' veteran Red Berenson, and Red Wings' sniper Mickey Redmond.

"It was unbelievably emotional, to the point where it was almost politics," said winger J.P. Parise, a player whose work ethic was far greater than his pure skill, which made him a surprise addition to the team, though he did not play opening night. "Me coming from a Minnesota town, especially during that time, I couldn't believe all the stuff involved. I had played eight or nine years outside Canada, and I'd forgotten how important the game was in Canada. There was an unbelievable feeling in that building that night."

"That first game, you didn't have to get the players up," said Ferguson. "They were ready, the adrenalin was flowing. And we went out and scored..."

Just thirty seconds into the game, Phil Esposito flipped

a Frank Mahovlich rebound over the fallen Tretiak to put the Canadians ahead, relieving whatever tension, maybe even doubts, that had existed.

At 6:32 of the first period, Henderson scored from the top of the faceoff circle, after Clarke had cleanly won a draw, to make it 2-0, and it appeared, as the scouting reports had suggested, and as almost everyone believed, the rout was on. All that was left was to see how bad it would get for the Soviets.

"We all knew what the scouting reports had said," remembered Sinden, "and for the first couple of minutes that's how it looked. They looked like an average team with poor goaltending. But I was still worried. The coach who's ahead 2-0 usually feels better than that. But even though we were up 2-0, you could tell it was going to be tough."

"I was prepared for the series, but I had no idea they had such a great team," said Henderson. "I can remember, even after we had scored the two goals, when I got back to the bench, I remember specifically saying that this was going to be a long, long series.

"I can also remember saying,'Oh, my gracious, have we got our hands full.' They were like a sleeping giant and there was a tremendously uneasy feeling. They were in incredible condition, composed, and they could skate and pass the puck so well. You just knew by the way they handled themselves, the way they skated, what kind of team they had."

"We all thought this would be easier than we'd thought," said Dennis Hull, who did not play this night. "And for those first six or seven minutes that's how it looked."

"When we got up by a couple of goals we were all saying,

'Here we go,'" said Peter Mahovlich. "Then, all of a sudden it was, 'There they go.'"

It was at about the midway point in the opening period that the Soviets began to relax, discovered their legs and began asserting themselves. At 11:40, little Evgeny Zimin took a pass from big winger Alexandr Yakushev and beat Dryden.

Before the period was over, nine seconds after defenceman Alexandr (Rags) Ragulin had been sent to the penalty box, Vladimir Petrov easily tapped a Mikhailov rebound past the fallen Dryden. End of one period, 2-2.

"At that point," said Henderson, "there was an absolutely sickening feeling."

"I remember the Russians had Montreal Surprise painted on their sticks," said Awrey. "It was like they knew what was going to happen."

"I went into the dressing room after the first period," said extra defenceman Bill White, "and everyone was just sitting around, and we knew we'd been duped. I mean, someone had made some serious scouting errors."

"I remember walking into the dressing room after the first period and talking to Yvon Cournoyer," said Marcel Dionne. "He just looked at me and said, 'You can't believe their strength and conditioning.'"

"When I got on the ice, it was already 2-0," said Gilbert. "Before I had even played my first shift it was 2-0, so I'm sitting on the bench saying, 'Let me on. Let me score my goals.' I figured it was going to 15, 17-0, and I wanted to score a few goals.

"Then I get on the ice and I didn't touch the puck the whole shift. The Russians started skating around with it, and I'm running around wanting to get the puck, and they wouldn't let me have the puck. Then they scored a few goals..."

Indeed, the Soviets never did let up. In the second period, fleet winger Valeri Kharlamov scored twice to give them what seemed a comfortable 4-2 lead. On the first goal, at 2:40, he deked around Awrey before squeezing a shot between the pads of a befuddled Dryden. Then, at 10:18, he fooled Dryden again with a forty-foot shot, which glanced in off the goalpost.

Suddenly the Soviets were ahead by two goals, after two periods, and an eerie silence fell in the Forum. The Canadians knew what lay ahead, and also knew they could do nothing to prevent the denouement.

"The biggest adjustment for us was the size of the rink," said Mikhailov. "It was much smaller than we were used to. But we just started playing our game. After we were down by two goals, we got the thought that we had nothing to lose. We knew we had to rush ahead, but the feeling was still bad until we scored.

"After tying the game 2-2, we knew we were starting to play our proper game. We got the feeling we could make it."

The Soviet domination was complete. They had mesmerized the Canadians with their strong, effortless skating; their deft, precision playmaking. And they were beginning to dominate because of superior conditioning. Beyond that, the Canadians hadn't ever seen such intricate pass patterns and persistent regrouping. The Soviets owned the puck, and they just plain confounded Dryden and his defence with their clever manoeuvring and shooting. The Canadians were being beaten at their own game, in their own rink.

Perhaps the key factor, though, was the Russians' crisp team play. They had been together in large part for months, the Canadians merely weeks.

"We were awed by what we were seeing," said Parise. "I really felt like an outsider, with the way the Russians handled the puck and the speed they had. I mean, we were all just thinking, 'Holy Cripes.' It was like the world was coming to an end."

Surprisingly, in the early minutes of the final period it seemed the Soviets lacked the killer instinct, or perhaps the determination that would become the trademark of this Canadian team. It would be proven a delicious bit of foreshadowing, too. Whatever, it became painfully clear that Tretiak was not the horrible goaltender everyone had been led to believe.

The Canadians arranged several excellent scoring chances early, a couple from Phil Esposito, another from Frank Mahovlich, but the young Soviet goaltender was at his acrobatic best, managing to further frustrate Team Canada.

Just when it was first beginning to seem hopeless, though, Clarke sliced the Soviets' lead to one goal — 4-3 — at 8:22, redirecting a shot by Ellis. A few minutes later, Cournoyer hit the post. That was as close as the Canadians would come on this night.

After Cournoyer's near miss, the Soviets proceeded up ice to effectively put the game out of reach. Mikhailov scored at 13:32, and just fifty-seven seconds later, with Team Canada beginning to fade, Zimin scored his second goal of the game. Yakushev concluded the scoring at 18:37.

Game over. Soviet Union 7, Team Canada 3.

"Holy shit, were we shocked," said Park. "But probably the most important thing that happened was some of the guys were trying not to let the others get down. They kept saying, 'Hey, we're going to win this thing.'"

"It was the best setup there's ever been," offered the injured Bobby Orr. "We got ahead 2-0 and we're all sitting in the stands laughing. Then all of a sudden, it's boom, boom, boom, boom…and holy shit, guys, what's happening here?"

"It was a shocker," said Dryden. "Even to those of us who should've known better, having played against the Soviets, it was a complete shock. I suppose we were a little overconfident. When you feel that way, you don't bother to look at the other team and see clearly what it has to offer. You begin to judge according to your own standards, so that if they skate differently you think that's not right, or if they shoot differently, you think that's not right. You tend to delude yourself."

It was apparent the Canadians had not only been duped by the Soviets, but perhaps also by themselves, believing that in nineteen days they could not only work themselves into satisfactory condition, but develop a team harmony, a oneness, on and off the ice.

"That series," said winger Wayne Cashman, "the Russians played a pretty good con game."

"That team had won four gold medals in the Olympics, and they were one of the best teams in the world," said Gilbert. "And then they showed the scouts the wrong goalie. They didn't show them Tretiak. I think that's cheating. When you go into a series, you've got to show what you've got."

But Team Canada was beaten in every area — in goal, on the blue line, up front, special teams. The Soviets had hit where it hurts most, too — pride.

"We just weren't a team," said Cournoyer.

"I don't think anyone on the team believed we were going to walk away with it," said Ellis, "but the players knew very quickly that the Russians hadn't come to learn, as they had told everyone. They had come to win."

Afterwards, there were some players simply overcome by shock. There were some who valiantly attempted to keep spirits raised, and still others who criticized the scouting report, blaming it in large part for their failings. Even seventeen years later.

"Well, it's obvious the Russians were no fools," said Dennis Hull. "They knew we would have someone there hanging around and watching, and there was no way they were going to show their best. I'm sure it was all planned out. But we should have known. I mean, we'd seen some of these guys before."

"We went in only knowing what we had been told," said Phil Esposito, "and that was that they weren't any good. Well, let me tell you that was one very good hockey team."

"It wasn't an easy loss to accept, but after the game we knew what kind of series it was going to be," said Peter Mahovlich. "You don't exactly get a chance to judge these teams too often, and we didn't know what to expect, not at all. But after that game, we knew we had our hands full. We knew it was going to be a great series."

It was that realization that was perhaps the only salvation from a shocking, thoroughly disappointing night for Team Canada. They weren't certain what they were up against when they started, were anything but respectful, and wound up being given an old-fashioned butt kicking, on home ice, before a worldwide television audience estimated at 100 million.

"The Russians kicked our ass that night," said Clarke. "Not only were we in shock, we didn't know what to think."

"It was a nightmare coming out of the Forum after that game," recalled Parise. "I mean, it was bad enough to lose to them, but losing in the Forum. Even my brother called me a bum."

"It was a tough night," concluded Sinden, "and a very difficult loss. But in two and a half periods, the Soviets did more than I was able to do in four weeks. I think that blowout finally convinced the players of everything I had told them."

"In the first period — by this time the fans recognized I was the interpreter," said Kukulowicz, "they came over to me and wished us a good series, but they said the Russians were going to lose. The score was 2-2. At the end of the game, they're calling me a goddamn communist."

"I'll never forget what happened in that game," said Eagleson. "We got ahead, but they just kept coming at us. Harry, Fergie and I were in total shock afterwards, but I remember Tommy Ivan and Sam Pollock walked into the dressing room and said, 'Well, boys, there are still seven games to go...'"

CHAPTER THREE

Redemption

It was the morning after a numbing night before. Standing at centre ice in Maple Leaf Gardens in Toronto, surrounded by his players and a decidely funereal atmosphere, Team Canada head coach Harry Sinden addressed his club for about ten minutes, the text of the speech focussing on restoring a somewhat shattered faith and confidence and reorganizing the game plan. The stunning 7-3 loss to the Soviets a night earlier in Montreal had understandably left his team devastated and confused.

Of all the scenarios, of all the predictions, of all the scouting reports, defeat — never mind the gut-wrenching, humiliating defeat with which they had to reconcile themselves that day — had never quite fit the equation.

And the second game, two nights later, was to have been for the purposes of driving another nail into the Soviets' coffin, to further confirm the Canadians' supremacy, not to rally for a night of uncertain vindication.

"I guess I had the players' attention by then," said Sinden.

"The important thing was to make sure the players didn't get too down, but were intent on redemption.

"And we decided to change some tactics. We practised early on the Sunday, the day after the Montreal game, and a big part of it was to change the tactics, to make sure we got everyone involved and got on the Russians early."

The game plan was, in essence, painfully simple. Forecheck with tenacity, liberate the Soviets from the puck and their many intricate flight patterns with the body, and generally be immensely more accurate around their goal, and decidedly more cautious around the Canadian net. Simple.

"Holy shit, were we in a state of shock," recalled defenceman Brad Park, a Toronto native. "We were pretty pissed off with what had happened. Yeah, humiliated. But the feeling of the team that day pretty much was, 'Let's get this second game going.' We couldn't wait to get back at them.

"Guys like Phil, Cash and Peter Mahovlich were always pretty vocal guys. They were sort of the leaders on the team, even then. And Fergie (assistant coach John Ferguson, who had carved a successful career with the Montreal Canadiens with grit and determination and toughness) was walking around telling everyone we were going to win."

Beyond making alterations to their strategies, Sinden and Ferguson also decided on several lineup changes, beginning in goal where Tony Esposito would replace Ken Dryden, who had surrendered the seven goals in the opening game. Eddie Johnston, the fifth goaltender named to the training camp roster a month earlier, but number three by tournament time, would serve as the backup.

Only allowed to dress nineteen players — seventeen skaters and two goaltenders — Sinden also changed his disbursement. Fully aware now, and much further aware than he would have preferred, of the Soviets' speed and, at that time in the series, superior conditioning, Sinden chose to dress a sixth defenceman for that game.

Deleted were Don Awrey and Rod Seiling, neither terribly fleet footed, although steady. Replacing them were Serge Savard, of the Montreal Canadiens, and the Blackhawks' reliable pairing of Bill White and Pat Stapleton. Brad Park, the surprising thirty-three-year-old Gary Bergman, and young Guy Lapointe remained from the opening night roster.

"I was surprised to play," said Savard. "I had missed the season before with a leg injury and had come back early. I was invited to camp because they didn't have enough players. I think Dallas Smith and Jacques Laperriere hadn't reported. When I went there, I thought I could play, but I didn't expect to.

"After we lost the first game, I was in the lineup the next game. If we'd won the first one, I probably would never have played. I think the biggest problem was we were overconfident. We weren't ready for them in the first game, but they were ready for us."

Up front, where the accent had now switched to intense forechecking and establishing a physical presence — not to intimidate, but simply to attempt to slow the Soviets, he insisted — Sinden added Chicago Blackhawks' veteran centre Stan Mikita, Boston Bruins' tough winger Wayne Cashman, and Minnesota North Stars' hard-nosed wingers J.P. Parise and Bill Goldsworthy.

Scratched were the New York Rangers' GAG (goal a game)

line of Rod Gilbert, Jean Ratelle and Vic Hadfield, along with Detroit Red Wings' sniper Mickey Redmond.

Sinden even rearranged lines, inserting Mikita between Yvan Cournoyer and Frank Mahovlich, thereby uniting Phil Esposito with Cashman, his Bruins' linemate, and Parise.

"We had to change the format," said assistant coach John Ferguson. "Coming to Toronto on the plane, you could've heard a pin drop. We had to do something, make changes. The GAG line had a couple of goals scored against them and we were thinking about the defensive game. We put big Peter in and he scored one of the great all-time goals."

The only unit to remain intact was the one that would ultimately become Team Canada's most consistent, the only one to remain together throughout the series, comprised of three players who were almost an afterthought when the final training camp roster was confirmed.

The pesky Bobby Clarke, as good at playmaking as he was at checking, centred Paul Henderson and Ron Ellis, two Toronto Maple Leafs returning home.

"It's funny," said Alan Eagleson, the team manager and a series organizer, "but the last three guys we picked for the thirty-five man roster were Clarke, Henderson and Ellis. And the last guy we picked, period, was Clarke. It was between him and Dave Keon of the Maple Leafs.

"I think Clarke had eighty-five points the season before, while Keon had something like forty-eight. Keon was experienced, a good skater and checker, but we decided to go with Clarke. People asked us, especially back then, do you think you made any mistakes selecting the team? I always told them, 'If we win the series, no. If we lose the series, yes.' But I don't think we made too many mistakes in picking that team."

The hands of fate and politics, of course, were both factors as significant in the selection process as any insights used or player preference. After all, forwards Bobby Hull and Derek Sanderson had taken the rich inducements of the upstart World Hockey Association and were ineligible to play. And Walter Tkaczuk, of the Rangers, could not break a commitment to work at a hockey school that summer. All three had originally been named to the thirty-five man roster and would have played in the series, at the very least at the start.

What if?

"I've never even thought about that," said Eagleson.

The lineup changes, though they ultimately proved to be successful, did reveal the first signs of dissension. When the players were initially commanded to serve their country, each player was promised by Sinden that he would play at least one game. Those who started in game one were reluctant to merely watch game two. And all the players invited remained with the team, for a while anyway. But after that first game, the realization that this series wasn't going to be easy came reluctantly, though wisely.

"We wanted to play everyone, and I promised all the players they would play in at least one game," said Sinden. "But it became pretty apparent we had to play our best guys to win it and I had to go back on my word. I didn't like it, but we had to win."

At that time, the morning of the second game, Sinden did not know just how necessary his paring of the roster would become, and it seemed the rearing of dissension's ugly head was somewhat premature, especially given the shocking result of the first game.

"We benched a lot of guys for that second game," said Eagleson. "That's when Vic Hadfield first started complaining. He argued he was one of the highest scorers in the NHL, a fifty-goal man the previous season, and he didn't need this.

"But I'll tell you, one of the guys I have the highest respect for is Rod Gilbert. I thought he might have been one of the guys we would have trouble with, but he never complained. And it eventually worked out well for him."

Gilbert was admittedly disappointed, perhaps even bitter, but he still managed to maintain his composure and hold back his complaints then and throughout the series.

"I didn't play in that game," recalled Gilbert. "They took our whole line off — Hadfield, Ratelle and me. We were one of the only lines that played together regularly in the NHL and they decided not to dress any of us.

"We felt like Sinden was blaming our line for what had happened. We all felt like we were being made scapegoats or something, and I really didn't like that. It was obvious, even then, that there were some problems already starting about who dressed and who didn't.

"I think Vic overreacted. Certainly he reacted a lot more strongly than Jean and I did. But I could accept the decision to go with different players. It was just that our line had had such a great year in the NHL.

"Vic just sort of said screw it after that, and he eventually did leave the team. Me? Well, I was still just happy to be there, to be a part of it all."

The most severe off-ice problems, born of those difficult roster decisions, would occur midway through the series. But there were other distractions. Outside of the immediate team, the second-guessing had begun, with the likes of National Hockey League president Clarence Campbell publicly questioning Sinden's roster selections for game one. Others doubted his strategy. And some 500 fans sent telegrams to the team, a solid majority of whom criticized the players for not remaining on the ice for the traditional — in international games, anyway — post-game handshake. The Canadians pleaded ignorance.

While bothered by public opinion, the team was otherwise consumed with more pressing matters, a second game and a very serious question of survival in the series.

Everyone was acutely aware that a loss by Team Canada that night, September 4, would have all but erased any real hope of winning this series, essentially placing them squarely in a position to salvage only a tie — at best. But a win, that would leave open the door for complete redemption. This one game, without question, would set up the rest of the series.

"You know, what happened that opening night probably was a blessing for us," said Johnston. "It sure didn't feel like it — not to us, not to the fans — at the time, but I think it wound up helping us.

"We discovered right off the bat what we were up against, that if we didn't get our act together and in one very big hurry, we would be in deep trouble. It took a while for that message to sink in, but we did learn. And it's like they always say, if you're going to lose you're better off getting it out of the way early."

"Even though we had just come off that emotional loss and

we were all in a complete state of shock, we still had confidence in our abilities and the talent on the team," said Cournoyer. "The biggest thing is we knew what to expect from them, and they really hadn't seen what our team had to offer."

But they soon would that night in Toronto, in what turned out to be Team Canada's most decisive victory of the series, a game in which the emotions would change from relief, to excitement, to quiet satisfaction. And in the end, redemption.

"There was nothing for the coaches, for anyone, to say before the game," continued Cournoyer. "Sure, we were all in shock, but we were all professionals and we had been in playoff situations before and that's what we were facing in that second game — a playoff situation.

"I remember once when I was playing in Montreal, we lost the first two games of a series against the Detroit Red Wings right in the Forum, but then we went out and won the next four games. But we knew what we had to do. We made the proper adjustments and did the job.

"This was the same thing. It was almost do-or-die for us, even though the series was still very young. But we knew we had to adjust and that's what the coaching staff stressed to us right up to game time.

"In the first game we didn't even know what the hell had happened to us, but afterwards we knew a lot more. It was a matter in the second game of putting all that to work."

Still, there existed in historic Maple Leaf Gardens that night more stifling pressure than excitement, though the support of the fans was staggering. In conservative Toronto, where the fans are generally quite reserved (even on the rare occasions when they actually have something to cheer about), on this night they stood as one and chilled the air singing the national anthem. But there also remained a sharp sense of trepidation, of apprehension. This sense no longer pertained to what the opposition would bring, but the home team.

It was seen in the corridor outside the dressing room, where goalie Tony Esposito paced nervously before the game.

"I get uptight before any game," said Esposito, "but this was worse."

The sometimes temperamental Frank Mahovlich had not talked to anyone the entire day, and seemed incredibly upset in the morning when he spotted some politicians being photographed wearing Team Canada uniforms. Two full hours before the game, the entire team was present in the dressing room, quietly preparing. Amid all that anxiety, however, both Sinden and Ferguson had an uncanny sense their players were ready.

"The pressure really was on us that night," recalled Johnston. "You could feel the tension everywhere. We just weren't supposed to trail by two games in that series and that was that. I remember Harry told us in the afternoon what was ahead for us. We knew it was going to take a great effort by all the guys to dig down deep and come up with the big one."

Remember, too, that what was at stake then and what became the overwhelming driving force for them to succeed was pride. This early in the series, it hadn't yet become an emotional political issue. The best players the NHL were allowed to assemble, playing under the name Team Canada, had been soundly beaten, and their pride had been deeply wounded. So, when they stepped on the ice that night for the second game in Toronto, they weren't playing for a doubting nation, but mostly for themselves. As a team.

"We were devastated," said Henderson. "This was supposed to be fun, but we were really hurting. We couldn't believe what had happened to us. It had started off as a lark, we were going to have a great time, then beginning that night it had suddenly become business."

"At that time, the series really wasn't important," said Parise. "No one knew how it was going to unfold. Everyone still was thinking we were the best team and that we would win. And most people just didn't know what to think after that first game. As the series grew, it became Canada versus Russia, a political thing, but it wasn't that way then."

If the atmosphere prior to game one was festive, it was deadly serious leading into game two. The tension was not to ease, either, until late in the game, although it was obvious from the beginning Team Canada was a vastly different team, playing with more composure and discipline, and perhaps even more purpose and determination.

"You can't play wide open and expect to win against the Soviets," said Billy Harris, former player and coach. "That's what went wrong in the first game."

So, the Canadians played a tighter, more controlled game, almost flawless in their defensive zone. They were also physical, the likes of Cashman and Parise and Goldsworthy unsettling and unnerving the Soviets with their thundering body checks. It might not have been a very popular plan of attack, at least not for the purists and the comrades, but it was undeniably effective.

The other major difference was in goal, where Tony Esposito

was brilliant, making a couple of excellent saves early, including one on the always dangerous Valeri Kharlamov.

"That night my brother, Tony, stood on his head, no question," recalled Phil Esposito. "He kept us in that game until we got our offence going."

After a rather bruising first period, which ended tied at 0-0, the Canadians opened the scoring on a delayed penalty at 7:14 of the second period. Phil Esposito freed the puck from the skates of a Soviet defender, swung from his backhand to his forehand in the slot, before beating a helpless Vladislav Tretiak, who had continued to impress.

Interestingly, Esposito had been tripped on the play and was sauntering back when the play broke before him. Park, and the imposing Cashman, assisted on the goal.

"Most guys take their time getting up and coming back to the bench, and they get heck from the coach," said Clarke. "But he takes his time and gets up and scores a goal."

End of two periods: Team Canada 1, Soviet Union 0.

Before the second period was over, too, Soviet defenceman Gynady Tsygankov was assessed a minor penalty. The frustration that had gripped the Soviets, essentially because of Team Canada's physical approach and in the comrades' opinion, the leniency of the officials, was beginning to show. While arguing the call and urging referee Steve Dowling to begin restoring order and give the Canadians penalties, Kharlamov bumped with the official, earning himself a ten-minute misconduct.

In the ensuing power play, just 1:19 into the final period, Park dispatched Cournoyer on a breakaway. He smoothly tucked a shot between the pads of Tretiak to put Team Canada ahead 2-0.

"They were more respectful of us in the second game," said Soviet centre Boris Mikhailov. "They understood we could play good hockey. They played very well, a very physical game. We had not seen such a style before."

The Soviets, though visibly disturbed, were still briefly able to make for a tense third period, when big Alexandr Yakushev emerged from a goal-mouth scramble and flipped a rebound over a prone Tony Esposito on a power play at 5:33, while Clarke was in the penalty box.

A feeling of déjà vu, one that would greatly intensify just twenty-one seconds later when Stapleton was given a minor penalty, was quickly beginning to sweep through Maple Leaf Gardens, the memories of a 2-0 lead lost in the opening game still frightfully fresh.

But that's when centre Peter Mahovlich rescued Team Canada by producing one of the single greatest plays, and goals, of the series. A supreme solo effort. Put into perspective, the dramatics of Henderson in game eight would not have been possible if not for the efforts of Mahovlich in the third period of game two.

With the Canadians shorthanded, the lanky centre, who had been relegated to fourth-line duty, mostly present to kill penalties, scored his truly memorable goal, barging past a Soviet defender, then deking over and around Tretiak at 6:47. The goal prompted an emotional rush for the Canadians, who emptied the bench in celebration.

"I could always remember the goal, but a few years ago I saw a videotape of it and was able to see the goal as it happened," said Mahovlich, who is now a special-assignment scout with the New York Rangers. Ironically, he was hired by Phil Esposito, the

Rangers' former general manager. "Phil got me a videotape of the series, a one-hour highlight package, and the goal is on it. I'll never forget that one. It was pretty special.

"It was a singular goal, a highlight in my career. We were up 2-1 and we were killing a penalty. They had just scored on a power play and there was a sense of, 'Here we go again, can we hang on?' It turned out to be a very key goal."

"It was a pretty goal and did we ever need it," said Phil Esposito. "Guy Lapointe had moved the puck up the boards to the blue line, and I passed it off the boards to centre, where Peter picked it up."

"I can still see that goal," said Henderson. "He was one-on-one with the defenceman (Evgeny Poladyev), and when he got to the blue line he faked the slapshot, pulled in the puck and froze the defenceman. Then he just barged through and reached around Tretiak to tuck the puck behind him. It was an absolutely incredible goal.

"That one put the icing on the cake for us. It was short-handed and put us ahead 3-1. If they score on the power play, we're up to our ears in it again."

Stunned by Peter Mahovlich's brilliance, the Soviets were, simply, done after that goal. Frank Mahovlich completed the scoring at 8:59. After Mikita stole the puck behind the net, he circled and centred to Mahovlich in the slot, who banked in a shot off the post.

Final score: Team Canada 4, Soviet Union 1.

In just forty-eight hours, a gritty bunch of Canadians had managed to restore their pride and, for the time being anyway, a precise order to the series. The individual talent had begun to impress, Phil Esposito emerging as the leader. The supporting cast, the likes of Clarke and Mikita, played significant roles, while Cashman and Parise thoroughly frustrated — and probably frightened — the Soviets with their relentless bumping.

"In that game," said journalist Dick Beddoes, "they inserted Cashman and he did what the Soviets hadn't seen too much of. He got his elbows up and scared the hell out of them. He was breaking all the rules of morality in hockey. All of a sudden, everyone's excited we've evened it up, but the moralists were outraged, saying we had to break the rules and put in a goon like Cashman to win. Cashman was horsewhipped by the editorial-page writers, not the jock writers. After that second game, it was us against them on the editorial pages."

As a team, they had dedicated themselves to close fierce checking, while Tony Esposito provided the calibre of goaltending they required to beat the Soviets. And in the third period, when conditioning might have again become a decisive factor, the Soviets could not solve the Canadian defence.

"That game saved our bacon," said Tony Esposito. "It was a real good game, one of the best. And we played a lot better, that's for sure. I played well in the first period, because if they had gotten us down early, I didn't like our chances."

"Harry corrected a few things and changed the lineup," said Park. "He changed the defence and everyone played well. He added Cash and Parise and Goldsworthy up front and made us a more physical team. The way the Russians were skating, we had to play physically and slow them down.

"As it worked out, it did help us. They were in much better condition and were such a good skating club, but we were able to slow them down. Before the game, Harry kept telling us we have to redeem ourselves. He said we were good enough to beat these guys and we were mad already. We had our motivation."

It was a team victory, too, just as the Soviets' was in the opening game. It was also decisive, Team Canada producing three goals in the third period when the issue was still in doubt, outshooting the Soviets, 36-21. It was so thorough a victory, in fact, that with about five seconds remaining in the game, having already glanced at the clock to check the time and convince himself that on this night it was all quite utterly hopeless, a Soviet defender showed his frustration and unwittingly played to the madly cheering crowd, flipping a shot toward his own net.

And for one glorious night, the torment Team Canada had endured for two days was at last relieved.

"You have to give Harry and Fergie a lot of credit," said Henderson. "Before that game we were all devastated, but they really got us regrouped. Game plan A was history, so let's take a look at game plan B. Our original plan was just to take it to them and see what happens. Well, we took it to them for about six minutes in the first game and saw what happened."

"That night," said Johnston, who had watched proceedings from the end of the bench, "we started to see the character we had on the team. The feeling was that once all the other aspects — the conditioning and getting used to playing with each other — came around, deep down we'd be okay. It was just a question of how long it would take, and no one had the answer."

"As a team we played much better, no question," said Sinden. "We played a disciplined game, but then we had a different lineup, too. We were a different type of team that night. It looked like we would get better after that game, too.

"I remember that after the game the players obviously were all very happy, and I was, too. But I knew it was still going to be a tough series. I congratulated the players afterwards, but I also cautioned them. "I just told them, 'Enjoy the victory, savour it, but there are still a lot of games to play.'"

Next stop Winnipeg...

CHAPTER FOUR

To Hull with Russia

There's an old line about brisk Winnipeg, one eventually credited to Team Canada reserve defenceman, witty Dale Tallon, who now works as a colour commentator for the Chicago Blackhawks' games on cable television. Anyway, the old line goes: Do you know who the athlete of the year has been in Winnipeg for the past ten years?

An ice fisherman.

Winnipeg can be an uncomfortable city in the summer, before the mosquitoes go south. And it can be quite unforgiving in the winter, when the snow and the mercury begin to fall. But on September 6, 1972, Winnipeg was pleasant enough. It could have been much worse, though. An unmitigated disaster.

While the spirits of Team Canada had been revived with their impressive 4-1 victory over the Soviets in game two in Toronto, the seeds of dissension were again beginning to sprout, and they would continue to grow. They were still a travelling party of thirty-five players then, after all, and a group of fifty in total, which meant the coaching staff had a wide variety of egos and temperaments to deal with. There was already some serious concern about playing time, or lack of it, and the roster decisions for the third game only added to the discontent.

"Heading to Winnipeg," said organizer Alan Eagleson, "everyone was feeling a lot better about our chances, but it was obvious some guys weren't happy. Vic Hadfield had already started to complain and was very sour. That almost became an infectious situation.

"I remember I sat next to Rod Gilbert on the way out to Winnipeg and, as I had said, I thought he might be one of the guys we would have trouble with. I thought he would be a guy who would complain. But Rod said to me he wanted to play as badly as the next guy, but why mess with a winning lineup? Two games later, he played the rest of the series."

Team Canada coach Harry Sinden, who had now been widely criticized for his deployment of personnel, and outwardly at least had remained unaffected, made just one lineup change for game three, scratching Minnesota North Stars' winger Bill Goldsworthy, who had dressed as an extra forward in the Toronto game, and reinstating New York Rangers' elegant centre Jean Ratelle, who had played in the opening-night loss with linemates Gilbert and Hadfield. The invitation that night, however, admitted just one.

"We were thinking defence," said assistant coach John Ferguson. "We had to have more checking on the wings, so we put in Parise. Everyone wanted to play and they were all worthy of it, but we had to make some decisions and we had to leave some guys out."

Sinden, who had found success using six defencemen, intended to adhere to that strategy and was not convinced he should dismantle his three forward lines, not after game two had shown they were just beginning to gel. Tony Esposito, impressive in his one appearance, remained in goal, backed up by Eddie Johnston.

"The roster was always decided on a day-to-day basis," said defenceman Bill White. "I wasn't told that I would play every game, but you still had to be prepared just in case you got the call. We were given enough time after the lineup was posted to get ready, to be prepared to play. But different guys reacted in different ways."

Whatever momentum they had gathered in Toronto, too, was tempered somewhat, because grave concerns about the red menace, the Big Red Machine, remained. Victory had been sweet, thorough and impressive, but it was also much more difficult than anyone had thought it would be. It took an exhausting, full-team effort, all cylinders firing, to solve the Soviets.

"I felt we were getting better, getting closer to where we wanted to be," said Sinden, "but we knew the Soviets would be tough. They had played their best game in Montreal and weren't quite as good in Toronto. Still, it was a tough victory. And I knew they would adjust for the third game."

Then there was controversy over the exclusion of superstar Bobby Hull, who was with the Winnipeg Jets of the rival World Hockey Association and so declared persona non grata for this series by the powers of Team Canada, which was born of an exclusive working agreement between the National Hockey League and Hockey Canada.

From the beginning, it was abundantly clear that no interlopers from the rich, new — rival — league would be welcome, and that included Hull, whose absence from Team Canada created an immense stir before the series, one that spawned contempt from the common fan and eventually involved Pierre Trudeau.

Hull, who had received a standing ovation at an afternoon luncheon the federal government gave the two teams, would watch the third game sitting in the stands among a sellout crowd of 10,600 at the Winnipeg Arena, flanked by Jets' owner Ben Haskins, who had rewarded him with an irresistible $2-million contract. Together, especially in Winnipeg, they made a regal portrait, as royal even as the huge picture of Queen Elizabeth that hangs on the wall at one end of the arena.

"It was a funny feeling sitting there," said Hull. "I'm still disappointed with what happened — that I couldn't play — and with the guys who stopped me from playing."

"Bobby Hull wasn't anything we could worry about at that time," said defenceman Brad Park. "There was still a tremendous controversy, what with the World Hockey Association and all, but there just wasn't any time for us to worry about it. We had enough on our minds."

Ironically, the Hull who was allowed to play, Chicago Blackhawks' winger Dennis, Bobby's brother, did not dress that night, either. But he at least was still a part of the team.

"Bobby understood why he wasn't playing for Team Canada," said Dennis Hull. "For him to play, all they had to do was ask. I don't think I would've been invited, either, if Bobby had been allowed. But the NHL was just trying to show how fair it could be by asking me to go along.

"What, I had scored thirty-nine or forty goals the year before? Look at some of the guys that were on that team. J.P. Parise, myself... we weren't the superstars. The NHL told the Canadian government anyone who played for the World Hockey Association couldn't play, and the Canadian government said fine.

"I wasn't going to go because of what was happening to Bobby, but he talked to me and convinced me that I should go. In hindsight, I'm glad I did. The problem, you see, was when we got the invitation it wasn't to try out, it was to play. There were thirty-five guys on that team, and you can't have thirty-five guys on a hockey team.

"That's why guys like Vic Hadfield, Jocelyn Guevremont and Gilbert Perreault were unhappy and eventually decided to leave. There were just too many guys around. It has only been in the subsequent series (in the Canada Cup tournament) that they have had tryouts."

To the historians of the day, Team Canada had appeared a rather weary team when they arrived in Winnipeg on the eve of game three, after a three-hour flight. Earlier in the day they had held a spirited workout in Toronto at Maple Leaf Gardens, and endured a delay upon arrival because of baggage problems. The fatigue, however, would not be seen until later the next night, as the third game in five days drew to a disappointing close.

* * *

"There was still quite a bit of pressure on us going into that game," said centre Peter Mahovlich. "It's funny, but it didn't matter where we went in Canada, the people didn't really understand we were playing for Team Canada. They kept relating it to the National Hockey League.

"People would look at Phil Esposito as coming from the Boston Bruins, and Brad Park as coming from the New York Rangers, and me as coming from the Montreal Canadiens. They had their favourites and they had guys they didn't like, and that's how they reacted. But at that time, they still really hadn't accepted us as being Team Canada.

"It made for a very uncomfortable situation at times, especially if we were having problems, which we were. It just wasn't very good, that's for sure."

Team Canada's plan of attack hadn't changed from the previous game. To be successful they required goalie Tony Esposito to be at his absolute best, they had to reduce the turnovers, and they had to continue to check relentlessly and bump the Soviets, who, as Sinden had predicted, had made some adjustments themselves.

Anxious to get all of their twenty-seven players some valuable ice time and experience, and undoubtedly concerned about the result of game two, the Soviet coaching staff of Vsevolod Bobrov and Boris (Chuckles) Kulagin made several lineup changes, inserting five fresh new faces.

Among them were three defenceman — Yuri Shatalov, Valeri Vasiliev and Vladimir Lutchenko. But they also resurrected the Baby Line, which was comprised of three university students, Viacheslav Anisin, Yuri Lebedev and Alexandr Bodunov. Their presence would prove to be quite significant.

Given the rigorous schedule, the travel, and the emotional and physical toll being exacted by the series, the Soviets' immense edge — superior conditioning and preparation — was to again become a decisive factor, especially with the addition of those young legs.

"In the second game, we had tightened it right up, and that's how we wanted to continue to play in the third game," said defenceman Bill White. "We were able to cope a lot better when it was that way."

"Back in Toronto, we had worked a lot on cutting off their breakouts," remembered Parise. "At that time, if you could break up their rush, they would circle back and try it over again. And when they had a power play, the point men would never shoot the puck. They'd try to make the plays from close in.

"So what we did was have one penalty killer checking the points, and the other three guys would be checking close to the net. We could afford to have that one guy out at the point because the point men never shot the puck.

"In the second game, they never really adjusted to what we did. But they started to change a bit in Winnipeg. But I think what really helped us in this series is that Harry was able to change things like that in between periods. So, we were able to adjust to things like that, where the Russians really wouldn't change anything. They had a way they liked to play, and they were reluctant to change it."

The pressure on Team Canada in this pivotal third game, the series knotted at a game apiece, was largely still an unfading residue of opening night. The second game had helped to ease the pain, but it would take at least another dominant victory — and probably more — to completely erase the memory of the shocking 7-3 defeat.

Just before the game, a moment of silence was observed for the eleven Israeli athletes killed by Arab terrorists in Munich at the Summer Olympics. The moment lent a much-needed perspective, a sense of reality, to proceedings. For this was, after all, just a hockey series. It wasn't life and death, although that would not be the overwhelming sentiment a few weeks later, or maybe even a few hours.

"Frank Mahovlich had watched on television everything that happened in Munich," said journalist Dick Beddoes. "He was a guy who was aware of more than just a hockey series going on in the world. There was at least a world beyond with Frank. He wasn't singleminded. But it affected him. I wrote about it, too. He thought the Russians were behind it. I think he psyched himself out."

The Canadians opened strongly that night, Parise scoring on a second rebound just 1:54 into the game. After White's point shot bounced off goalie Vladislav Tretiak, Parise shot once, then a second time, before scoring. They adhered to their plan of bumping the Soviets, too, the line of Paul Henderson, Ron Ellis and Bobby Clarke extremely effective. But belligerent Wayne Cashman, who had incurred the wrath of the Russians for his abrasive behaviour in the second game, was closely scrutinized by the officials this time, and he earned a couple of minor penalties for slashing before finally being banished from the game midway through the final period for arguing a call. This undoubtedly delighted the Soviets.

Bobrov, the co-coach, had said before the game that, had Cashman been playing in Europe, he would have spent the entire game in the penalty box. His efforts unsettled the Soviets in the second game, but were decidedly less effective this night, the Soviets maintaining deportment and discipline.

Anyway, the Soviets tied the game a few minutes later with their third shorthanded goal of the series. Frank Mahovlich was guilty this time of a misguided pass at his blue line, and Vladimir Petrov quickly turned it into a goal. It was the sort of unforced error Sinden had hoped to avoid.

"We just couldn't afford to give the Russians anything," recalled Sinden. "It was tough enough, and they don't miss too many chances."

"It took a while for us to learn," said Cournoyer, "but they were dangerous even when they were shorthanded. They never stopped coming at you."

Before the period was over, though, Ratelle had given the Canadians another lead, converting a perfect pass from Cournoyer, while Tony Esposito proceeded to preserve the lead with a stunning variety of tough saves.

End of one period: Team Canada 2, Soviet Union 1.

In the second period, their lead would swell by one, with Cashman doing some effective work in the corners and centring to big Phil Esposito at 4:19. It appeared, again, that Team Canada was sitting comfortably, playing well enough, and in command. But memories of other leads simply refused to die.

"I just didn't have a good feeling," said Sinden.

Midway through the period, the Soviets trimmed the lead to 3-2 with another heartbreaking shorthanded goal. Valeri Kharlamov, the speedy winger, got behind Park and easily beat Esposito.

Just fifty-one seconds later, though, Henderson would use his speed to win a foot race with defenceman Alexandr Gusev, and the lead was again at two — 4-2. But that would be it for Team Canada.

"We were ahead 4-2 and hadn't played that badly," recalled Sinden, "but we hadn't played that well, either. We had no reason to be ahead. One of the toughest things in hockey is that the score usually dictates how the team feels, and we were ahead, so our team felt very good about itself. But they were feeling good when they probably shouldn't have. I remember, I was still a little bit worried."

In less than four minutes, Sinden's fears were realized and the Soviets had tied the score, 4-4, the gamble by the Soviet coaching staff to audition its Baby Line paying off rather handsomely.

First, Lebedev deflected a point shot from Vasiliev past a confused Esposito at 14:59. Then, at 18:28, Bodunov accepted a centring pass from Anisin to score his first goal of the series.

End of two periods: Team Canada 4, Soviet Union 4.

"They put out that young line we hadn't seen before and they dominated us," said Sinden. "In the third period, we were actually quite fortunate to finish in a tie. It ultimately turned out to be a big point, too."

In that third period, the Canadians began to noticeably tire and fade, chasing but not catching the Soviets, who obviously had much more in reserve, in particular its young forward line. Team Canada was only outshot 8-6, but relied on Esposito — and a game-saving sweep of a loose puck by Park — to keep them alive, particularly in the final ten minutes when the bumping and intense checking had ceased.

For the Soviets, twenty-year-old goalie Vladislav Tretiak continued to frustrate the Canadians and for the second consecutive game was selected their player of the game. Henderson was chosen the Canadians' most valuable player, and nearly did produce the winning goal in the frantic final period, but was robbed by Tretiak's quick glove hand.

Where the Canadians had suffered most, though, was in handling and adjusting to the Soviets' fast break. They are masters of the transition game, switching quickly from defence to attack. And opposing defencemen pinching in at the blue line, taking unnecessary chances, usually pay dearly for their indiscretion. At their own blue line, the Canadians had to adapt to the Soviets' detailed pass patterns.

"The big difference," said Park, "was in reading the play. You know, if your wingers picked up the loose man, then the defence was all right. But you also really had to show some patience because of their style, criss-crossing the ice and dropping passes all the time.

"As long as we had the style of never giving up our blue line, which meant the wingers were picking up the loose man, we were all right. See, in the NHL back then, you never gave up the blue line. So when the Soviets made their drop pass, it would be outside the blue line and they wouldn't be able to penetrate. But we didn't always hold that line."

After the game, in a rare display of humour, Soviet co-coach Bobrov wondered aloud at the press conference what his young goalie would do with all the rings he was winning as the game star.

"He just got married, so he will probably keep one and give

the other to his bride," said Bobrov that night. "And with the third, fourth and fifth? His former girlfriends might be honoured."

The Canadians, meanwhile, had the distinct feeling of being bridesmaids. This was their party and the Soviets were ruining it. Spirits were not good. They had allowed two leads to disappear, had again seen the maddening effects of their poor conditioning, and there were more ripples of dissension, this time with Richard Martin, Buffalo Sabres' young forward, expressing his discontent.

"We got ahead, let a lead slip away, but that just drove the point home again," said Cournoyer. "No matter if we were on a power play or playing even strength, the Russians were always dangerous. Sometimes, though, it just takes a while to sink in.

"But the big problem was we still weren't a team. We were having problems on the ice, some guys were complaining about not playing, and we always seemed to have a different lineup each game, using two or three different players. It just never seemed to work as well as it could."

Time, obviously, was the only remedy for what ailed Team Canada. But at that point, time they didn't have. Misery, yes. Doubters, yes. Dissenters, yes. But time, no.

"Everyone called us Team Canada, but I don't think you could've called us that then," said Awrey. "You can take a bunch of guys and put Team Canada on their sweaters, but it's not really Team Canada. When the Russians play a series like that, they've practised together for months and months, and really are a team. So when we got put together, it wasn't really a well-oiled machine."

Even though they had survived with a tie, looking back, the sensation and emotion seemed more like a loss. And at the time, they had an eerie feeling of impending doom.

"When we got to Winnipeg, we felt pretty good about ourselves," said Eagleson. "We had played a great game in Toronto and figured we could build on it. I think everyone thought the team was finally coming together.

"We did play well enough early in the third game, but afterwards we were all depressed again. We had been ahead 4-2 and allowed them two shitty goals."

Next stop Vancouver...

CHAPTER FIVE

"We're doing our best..."

I t was a bewildered Team Canada who arrived in Vancouver the next afternoon, the series deadlocked. It was becoming increasingly apparent, too, that the support of the country was beginning to waver as the supposed myth of their hockey superiority continued to be destroyed. Being tied in the series just wasn't quite good enough. Team Canada was supposed to have flexed its broad muscles and the Soviets were supposed to have reeled in fear and inferiority.

The frustration and disappointment would never be any greater than on September 8, 1972, at the solemn Pacific Coliseum, where in an utterly bizarre turn of events, a humiliating defeat would ultimately become a revival session of sorts, doing what four games, a month of days together, and a coaching staff could not. It was the night, when the game was over, that Team Canada became a team.

"It was a strange night," said reserve goalie Eddie Johnston.

"We thought we should've won the third game in Winnipeg, but all things considered we were happy with the tie. We had no idea before the fourth game how the public felt, how they would react. We just knew we had to win that next game."

The news leading up to it was almost an omen of what was to follow. The news was all bad. The morning of the game, after a light workout, it was discovered that rock-steady defenceman Serge Savard, of the Montreal Canadiens and now their managing director, had suffered a hairline fracture of his ankle after stepping in front of a shot by teammate Red Berenson.

"I was so disappointed," said Savard. "I didn't think I would play in the series, but I got a chance. Then this happened. I wasn't having much luck. But I decided to stay with the team and go overseas. We had ten days off and that really helped me."

Savard was listed as being "through for the series, and on an excruciatingly personal level, it appeared an absolutely crushing setback in his hard-luck career. Twice previously he had broken his left ankle during National Hockey League seasons.

Savard's defence partner, Guy Lapointe, was also unable to play, having been shaken up and bruised the previous game after a forced collision with the endboards. Perhaps the steadiest defence pairing Team Canada possessed had been dissolved.

In their place, Don Awrey and Rod Seiling returned to the lineup. Neither had played since the fateful opening-game loss. The other defencemen were Bill White and Pat Stapleton, Brad Park and Gary Bergman, all holdovers from the first game.

Dryden hadn't played, either, since the shocker in Montreal, but he started the fourth game, backed up by Johnston. Many questioned Sinden's decision, given Dryden's ordinary effort in the opener and the brilliance with which Esposito had played the past two games. But Sinden was insistent he required two goalies to win the series, though the Soviets were managing quite nicely with one, the splendid young Vladislav Tretiak.

"The mental and physical preparation in that series was so great," explained Sinden, "we just felt we would be better served using both goalies, keeping them fresh. The mounting pressure in that series was unbelievable. It became exasperating at times."

Sinden had continued to feel extreme heat and hear volumes of second-guessing for most of his decisions, pretty much standard behaviour when a team is supposedly underachieving, and particularly when the coach had happened upon a winning combination two games earlier but chose to break it up.

True, the realignment on defence for the fourth game had been forced on him, but Sinden also virtually overhauled the forward lines, making five changes.

His first was the addition of Buffalo Sabres' flashy centre Gilbert Perreault, who replaced Stan Mikita between Frank Mahovlich and Yvon Cournoyer, while Phil Esposito was given a pair of new wingers — Minnesota North Stars' rugged Bill Goldsworthy and Chicago Blackhawks' big shooter Dennis Hull. They substituted for Wayne Cashman and J.P. Parise. Sinden also scratched Peter Mahovlich and Jean Ratelle, replacing them with Rangers' wingers Vic Hadfield and Rod Gilbert. For Perreault and Hull, it was their first action in the series, and both would make significant contributions.

The Soviets, meanwhile, made two alterations on defence, bringing back veteran Alexandr (Rags) Ragulin and Evgeny

Poladyev. They also swapped a couple of fourth-line forwards, and these lines remained pretty much intact for the rest of the series. That meant the Baby Line of Anisin, Bodunov and Lebedev, which so dominated the third game, remained.

"Sinden put us, Hadfield and me, into the lineup with a couple of other guys," said Hull of his series debut, a move he now questions. "Sinden was trying to get the guys in, but sometimes it's better to stay with the original lineup. They know better what to expect, and how to play against them.

"The guys (who had previously played) just said to us, 'You can't win this by yourself.' That made me feel good. When you look at it that way, it takes the pressure off, so you just go out there and play your game. I played a pretty good game, too, got lucky and scored a goal. But for the team it wasn't a very good night."

The lineup changes might have appeased some, but they were doing absolutely nothing to develop any sort of continuity. But then, the presence of thirty-five players was a mistake they could not anticipate or easily rectify — and have never repeated.

"When you change your lineup all the time, putting four or five new players in, it's tough to play as a team," said Cournoyer. "And we still weren't in shape, not to play the Soviets. Everyone was trying so hard, but nothing was working. That's what happened that night."

News hounds were provided with a welcome diversion prior to the game — from Toronto Maple Leafs' owner Harold Ballard, who back then was a major ally of Eagleson and summit series. Ballard was overheard offering the Soviet delegation $1-million for winger Valeri Kharlamov. Today, Ballard will not even allow

Soviets into his hockey rink, neither hockey players nor circus performers. Ironically, on the day Ballard was being so loose with his money, the day before game four, he originally was supposed to have been appearing in court in Toronto on charges of stealing from Maple Leaf Gardens, Ltd. But the series had so gripped the nation, the sentencing was postponed until October 20.

* * *

It took precisely 121 seconds before Team Canada would fully comprehend just how bugged and bothered the Canadian public was with their performance in the series. This disenchantment was relayed by some 15,700 unhappy fans at the Pacific Coliseum.

"Vancouver fans are funny," said Dick Beddoes. "They eat their young."

The initial target of the fans' wrath was Goldsworthy, but he soon would have some very select company. At just 1:24 of the first period, the big winger was assessed the first of two minor penalties, both of which ended with Soviet centre Boris Mikhailov redirecting point shots from defenceman Vladimir Lutchenko behind Dryden.

The first goal arrived at 2:01, accompanied by a small smattering of discontent. With the second at 7:29, the booing began to become rather lusty.

End of one period: Soviet Union 2, Team Canada 0.

"The refereeing was bad," said Henderson, "and we did take some foolish, stupid penalties. They got those two quick power-play goals and we're down 2-0 right off the bat. Then we opened it up, and they'll eat you for lunch when you do that."

"It was obvious," added Johnston, "the fans weren't completely with us in this one."

Between periods, Sinden decided he would give the speedy Perreault more ice time, hoping his skating might create a chance or two. At worst, he could keep up with the Soviets. Early in the period, at 5:37, Sinden's decision proved wise, as Perreault scored a beautiful goal, capping off an electrifying end-to-end rush.

Perreault picked up the puck in the Canadian zone, weaved through a crowd of players in the neutral zone, powered around the Soviet defence, circled the net and happily watched his centring pass carom off a sliding Vasiliev and behind a startled Tretiak.

"For me, it was the highlight of the series," said Perreault.

The effects of Perreault's exciting goal were painfully short-lived, however. The Soviets restored their two-goal lead just fifty-seven seconds later. With Stapleton caught up ice after his shot had been blocked at the blue line, and only White back to defend, Yuri Blinov successfully completed a sharp two-on-one break with Vladimir Petrov, easily tapping a pass behind Dryden.

Later in the period, the Soviets began to thoroughly dominate, forcing the frustrated Canadians to scamper carelessly about their zone. One particular sustained attack produced their fourth goal at 13:52, Vladimir Vikulov scoring from the slot with three Canadians flailing aimlessly in the corner. The price was steep for the Soviets, though, with Vikulov suffering a shoulder injury on the play.

End of two periods: Soviet Union 4, Team Canada 1.

And the booing got louder...

"That game wasn't much of a show," admitted Sinden. "We hadn't played well in the games before and we weren't playing well that night. The difference was our luck didn't hold out in that game the way it did in Winnipeg, and we got thumped by them."

"We stunk the joint out," said Eagleson.

Goldsworthy, the target of the fans' contempt early in the game, partially redeemed himself at 6:54 of the third period, whacking Phil Esposito's rebound past Tretiak, who was again chiefly responsible for the Soviets' maintaining their lead. While overall an undistinguished effort by the Canadians, the team did rally briefly after the Goldsworthy goal, outshooting the Soviets 23-6 that period, but they could not beat the young goalie. Overlooked in the vast criticisms of Team Canada, at that point in the series anyway, was the splendid work of Tretiak. The fans, it seemed, only remembered hearing he would have difficulty stopping a beach ball.

At 11:05 of the third period, Vladimir Shadrin effectively put the game out of reach, breaking the Canadians' spirits, sliding in his own rebound. Hull completed the scoring with just 22 seconds remaining.

Final score: Soviet Union 5, Team Canada 3.

And the booing got louder...

It was neither a festive, nor pretty scene at the conclusion of the game. The first half of the series was now officially in the record books, the upstart Soviets were leading in games, 2-1-1, and looked to be in complete command with the final four games to be played in Moscow.

It didn't matter that the Soviets had proven themselves a worthy opponent, either, underrated and unappreciated. In the eyes of fans, Team Canada had been underachieving, it had let them down, by playing abysmally and not upholding the honour of the country. Hockey is, after all, a bragging right with Canadians. All that mattered was thrashing the Soviets and it wasn't happening. They didn't want reasons, they wanted results. And suddenly it had all become much more than just a hockey series. Our heritage, our national pastime was being stolen. A country's fragile confidence and pride was being broken.

"That was a bad one, too," said Dryden. "I think the anger and the disappointment of the fans really began to show. It was a bad night, and in the next week or so it became just as bad or worse a time in Sweden. The reason the Vancouver fans felt so bad is that it seemed as though it had all slipped beyond us. Leaving Canada with a deficit was just plain bad."

"I really think the people in Vancouver forgot this was still a hockey game," said Cournoyer. "But I guess it had become more than that. But the people were also wrong to boo us. It's not like we went out there to lose."

"It was a shock the way the Canadian people treated us," agreed Cashman. "The public, and us, were both misled. Everyone sort of had the impression it was a pickup game against a bunch of Russian amateurs. But these guys were more professional than the National Hockey League. Their whole life is built around this hockey team and they had been waiting twenty-five years to play Canada.

"The pressure was tremendous. We went into it looking at it as a fun series. The Russians, they were out to prove they had the superior system. The hockey was secondary. It was all political."

It took Phil Esposito, who had become the spiritual and physical leader of the team, to put it all into sharp perspective, to share with the public the feelings and frustrations of the players, and their disappointment, but also to get off their collective chest the hurt they were feeling, the sense of betrayal.

Harsh words were required, and an emotional, brutally honest Esposito delivered them in an impassioned speech during a post-game television interview. It would ultimately serve as the turning point for Team Canada, a gathering of their spirits. If they suddenly felt abandoned, left alone to continue the fight in ten days in Moscow, then they would damn well do it together.

"To the people across Canada, we're trying our best," Esposito told a nationwide television audience that night. "The people boo us. We're all disappointed, disenchanted. I can't believe people are booing us. If the Russians boo their players like some of our Canadian fans — not all, just some — then I'll come back and apologize.

"We're completely disappointed. I can't believe it. We're trying hard. Let's face facts. They've got a good team. We're all here because we love Canada. It's our home and that's the only reason we came."

Seventeen years later...

"I hadn't seen the tape of that for five or six years, honest to God," recalled Esposito. "I couldn't remember what I had said. But I remember it bothered me. We were working our butts off in that series and getting booed. I didn't like it at all, not so much that they were booing me, but my teammates, the team.

"Shit, man, they gave up on us. And the media wasn't very nice to us, either. What people didn't realize is you could take a junior team now, play them against the New York Rangers tonight. If they could be together five or six years to get ready, they could win the game in a one-shot deal.

"Everyone was saying we should be killing those guys, but nobody knew how well they could play, and we weren't in the greatest of shape for what we had gotten ourselves into."

"Phil came back to the dressing room afterwards," said Henderson, "and I was sitting next to him. I remember he said, 'Well, I really told the people off.' That was the sign of a great leader. I mean, leaders do whatever has to be done at the time. He went out and did what had to be done."

Till then, there had been something of a leadership void on Team Canada, but Esposito had boldly stepped forward and taken charge.

"They booed Canada that night," said Beddoes. "But without Bobby Hull and Bobby Orr, I think there was a leadership vacuum. Phil filled the void. After the game, he grabbed a sweater and asked why Canadians were booing them, booing the Maple Leaf. He had suddenly become the leader.

"Hull, of course, had been blackballed. Many people said if he was there, he would've gotten the slapshot up around Tretiak's ears and it could've made a difference. We were missing Orr, too. I think Hull would've been the leader on that team. It's ironic, as it turns out, a lot of us back in training camp thought Phil was a bum. He'd just come off a big year in Boston, but he was late arriving at camp. Eagle said, and I wrote it, that he was a money grabber staying back at his hockey school. But he turned out to be the leader. He proved a lot of us wrong."

"It's like Phil said that night, we were trying our best," offered Cournoyer. "And they were a damned good hockey team. Don't forget, people are still talking about the Russian players — Tretiak, Yakushev, Kharlamov — seventeen years later. Sometimes people forget there are two teams on the ice."

"What was hard was the reaction around the country, what happened that night in Vancouver," said Park. "And they were just killing us in the newspapers. Oh boy, it was one big kettle that was boiling. We knew that we were giving it our best."

But it was also clear that not only was their ability being doubted, but their integrity and sincerity. They had been cast in the role of traitors for not upholding the honour. The series, at its outset, hadn't unfolded as most had been brainwashed to believe, and it had become the rage not to support, but criticize and ridicule. Kick 'em when they're down. And the derivative of fan is...fanatic.

"It had gotten to the point where we were going to win it for ourselves," said Parise. "After all that bullshit in Canada, out in Vancouver, we sort of thought to ourselves, 'Well, screw you. We'll win this thing for ourselves.'"

"The fans in Vancouver were really tough on us," said Ratelle. "But you've still got to go out and play. Espo's speech sort of reflected how we were all feeling that night. At that time, we knew we were going to Russia behind the eight ball, and we sort of felt we had to do well, or win, whether the fans got behind us or not. He just let them know that we were trying."

"Maybe the fans' reaction that night was a reflection of the attitude across the country," said Johnston. "I don't really know. But the guys certainly didn't need to hear all that booing. What was going on, well, it was frustrating for everyone, but it was especially frustrating for the guys on the ice.

"What people forgot was we weren't just the home team out there. We were representing our country, representing *them*. To boo guys who were representing your country, well, it would be like booing an army. And this was war, basically. That's how we looked at it."

And war is hell.

"There was that business with the fans," began Eagleson, who vowed then never to allow another international game in Vancouver and kept his promise until the 1984 Canada Cup, when he made the same declaration after poor attendance for a Team Canada-Team Sweden game. "Phil gave his impassioned speech, and then we go to Sweden and there was almost open revolt."

Next stop Stockholm for a pair of exhibition games, then Moscow...

CHAPTER SIX

To Russia with Luck

"By the time we left Canada, we felt like we had been literally deserted, and it somehow got worse when we got over to Sweden," remembered Team Canada head coach Harry Sinden.

The crowd of non-travellers at Toronto International Airport on the night of September 12 was pathetically small, consisting of family, a few friends, and even fewer fans. This wasn't goodbye, it was good riddance.

Four days after they had been thrashed in Vancouver before a hostile crowd apparently representing the views of the country's hockey fans, a beleaguered, confused and depressed Team Canada was bound for Stockholm, Sweden, for two exhibition games. They were designed to familiarize the team with the many nuances of European hockey, the bigger ice surface, abysmal officiating, sneaky dirty tactics of the European players, and such. But it was also to be another colossal test of their character and resolve, an acid test of the chemistry of the team.

At that point, Team Canada was confronted and more than a

little confounded with the staggering reality of having to defeat the impeccable Soviets in Moscow three times to win the series and preserve their dignity. At customs, they sheepishly declared that they trailed 1-2-1. They had played a distinguished team they had terribly underestimated, a team in superior condition, and on even terms a worthy opponent. The Soviets were good, the Canadians had not yet reached that point, and there were serious doubts as to whether they ever would.

Still, when they left Toronto that night, they remained steadfastly defiant, insistent they would win their summit series, but hope appeared only faint. By the conclusion of the first four games in Canada, the fans had grown thoroughly disenchanted with this team. They had felt let down, betrayed. It's ironic, but that was how the players felt, too, their sentiments voiced in Esposito's stirring speech.

They were words that originated directly from the heart and would ultimately come to rest there, reviving the spirits of a team whose perhaps biggest failing had been its failure to achieve a feeling of oneness, a togetherness.

"But when we left Vancouver, we were determined to do whatever was humanly possible to win the series," recalled winger Dennis Hull. "We wanted to show these people that we could do it."

Dryden added, "I don't remember thinking, 'Here we go, or it's gone.' I may have at the time, but I really don't have a recollection."

But, typical of their existence that first ten days, before Team Canada could take one big step forward, it regrettably had to take two steps backward. The latest setback took place in Stockholm, where they played the Swedish national team, which had a history of seamy confrontations with Canadian national teams. The Swedes were not interested in merely serving as sparring partners for the Canadians, but were intent on taking full advantage of their time on the world stage to make a name for themselves, and share the spotlight.

"Getting off the aircraft in Stockholm, Cashman says, 'Where were you guys in World War II?'" recalled Dick Beddoes. "The remarks got published in the papers over there and the next night in the game..."

The result was a couple of absolutely brutal exhibitions, the first game won by Team Canada 4-1, the second ending in a 4-4 tie and bloodshed, the Canadians' lack of composure and the antagonism of the Swedes leading to utter mayhem. The ugliest of the incidents involved Cashman. He had a confrontation with the stick of winger Ulf Sterner, who had a brief stint in the NHL and emerged from it with a severely lacerated tongue. The main Swedish casualty was defenceman Lars-Eric Sjoberg, whose face with its broken nose was splashed across the pages of the local newspapers the next morning, under headlines that portrayed the Canadians as international hooligans.

The Swedish press was cruel in its criticism of Team Canada for its part in the imbroglio, absolving the home team of any blame. But it was probably no harsher than the touring Canadian media, which sent similar dispatches back home to a horrified and disgusted public. This was doing nothing to foster support, of course. Not only had Team Canada, in the estimation of a solid majority of fans, disappointed them against the Soviets, but while in Sweden they were also scuffing the country's fine image abroad.

"Like I said, we were literally deserted by the fans, by the media, plus by every Canadian back home, the ones interested in sports or otherwise," said Sinden. "We found ourselves regarded almost as traitors, like we had let the entire country down in some way.

"There were fifty in our party and we were on our own. That's how we felt. We certainly weren't held in terribly high esteem, but that seemed to have an effect on the team. Maybe it brought us together.

"We had a meeting in Sweden that Al and I conducted on that subject — that we had been left alone and we were going to sink or swim alone in this series."

Actually the meetings were far more involved, as were the problems. They were far more acute than a simple feeling of rejection. There continued to be turmoil within the team, some players still not happy about their lack of playing time, while others questioned the degree of commitment of their teammates. Then there was the really serious matter of whether the wives would be allowed to bunk with their husbands in Moscow, if they were invited at all.

"In Sweden," said team manager Eagleson, "there was open revolt. Some of the guys didn't think we had a chance of winning and there was the typical moaning and groaning. So I went to the coaches and I said 'We've got two days left in Sweden.' I told them to assemble the entire travelling party — no reporters — in the restaurant and I gave them a lecture.

"There were fifty people in the room. By then even the doctors were yapping and complaining. The doctors! I told everyone in that room, 'We've got ourselves a leaky boat and it looks like we're sinking. If you don't want to do it, then get the hell out. If you don't have the attitude we're going to win, then leave.'"

At that point, no one departed, although the players had decided to convene an impromptu meeting of their own to discuss several pressing matters that had been troubling them. Naturally, it was chaired by the team leader, Phil Esposito, who was only just beginning to vent his concern and display his determination. The night in Vancouver was only the beginning, the meeting in Sweden a continuation. The best was to come on the ice in Moscow.

"Playing those games there (Sweden) helped us get used to the bigger ice surface," said Park. "But there were some other problems, too. We heard the Soviets had put all the wives in one hotel and all the players in another, so we said we weren't going. It was just adding fuel to the fire.

"Then when we were playing the Swedish nationals we were criticized for our rough play. Even the Canadian consulate, the Ambassador to Sweden, condemned us for our style of play."

"I remember being in the cafeteria in Sweden and we were told by Eagle, Harry and Fergie that they didn't want our wives to come with us," remembered Phil Esposito. "At that point, I asked them to excuse us, and we had a team meeting and we just decided, well, they need us more than we need them right now.

"We just said if they don't let the wives come over, then to hell with it all. We'll go home, and everyone in the room agreed. Then we called them back in the room and Al just says, 'Well then, go for it guys.' But that was the first time the guys had all stuck together. I firmly believe that's when we started coming together as a team."

"That was the turning point," said centre Marcel Dionne, who hadn't yet played. "That's when we realized this thing was for real, when we got away over there. I was only twenty years old, but I remember telling Phil they're good players and they're going to beat us. He was so mad at me, I was almost under the table. But that's how much he was into it. He convinced me we were going to win. He wasn't going to let us lose."

"I agree, I think the turning point was the getting together in Sweden," said winger J.P. Parise. "When we went over there, it seemed everybody was against us, but I think that brought us all a lot closer together as a team.

"That week between games, we went out and we knew what we had to do to win. We had to upgrade our conditioning, but we were also finally getting to know each other. We would go for dinner, or go for walks together, or for a few beers.

"I guess you could say we developed a social life and began to appreciate each other. We had one goal and we started going at it as a group, instead of going in twenty different directions. We had accepted everybody's contribution and appreciated each other's goal.

"You have to remember, too, back then in the NHL, you didn't have friends on the other teams. When you were picked by a particular team, you became a part of that team through your career. You know, sometimes you would have a friend on another team, but when you got on the ice it was war. You didn't stand around talking to the guy like they do sometimes today.

"So when they picked Team Canada, you put all these guys

together, and they have had fights and mean words back in the NHL, and some guys hold grudges."

"By all appearances it was a destructive time," recalled Dryden. "We played poorly and got an absolutely terrible reception from the Swedish crowds. The games were sloppy, chippy, petulant and sour. Perhaps it was positive only in the sense that we got a feeling that there's nobody else out there, that we had no allies. Maybe through that there was a positive effect on the team."

Sinden was also credited with having a profound influence on the team, guiding them through these difficult, emotional times. "He was a brilliant coach," said Dennis Hull. "To get us back to where we could win the series in Moscow, like he did, was one of the best coaching feats ever. He was a good psychologist, a good observer. He knew by going to Sweden we'd be exposed to some of the differences of playing over there. Most of the guys had never played against the Europeans, and things are very different over there. You'll have players spitting and kicking, but we're not used to that in the NHL.

"Behind the bench, Sinden was always in complete control. I remember in Sweden, we had played those two games and we were getting on the plane to go to Russia, and Harry said to me, 'This is going to be tough, but we're a team now. We're going to win this thing in Moscow.'"

"In Toronto during training camp," said Clarke, "we had guys running back and forth to hockey schools and what not. It wasn't that we weren't taking the series seriously, but everyone thought it was going to be a lark. But over in Sweden we started to get a lot closer."

This newfound togetherness, allegiance and sense of purpose was to be interrupted a few days later, however, after Team Canada had touched down in Moscow, greeted by their wives, team officials and some 2,700 Canadian loons, who had paid thousands of dollars to spend a week in Moscow, support their team, and witness history.

"The way Ballard put it," recalled Beddoes, "he said the wives had come over with mattresses strapped to their backs."

It was also, obviously, the first time the players had ever seen Moscow, a huge city that is alarmingly backward by North American standards. Then, there was a lineup for virtually everything — food, gas, drink. A lineup just to lineup. And the players' knowledge of the country was, well, essentially limited to any spy novels or Smirnoff bottles they might've devoured.

The people are actually quite polite, though quiet and reserved. In September the weather can be dreary, not unusually cold, but dank and overcast. It quite simply wasn't the most pleasant place to be, the food horrible, the water leading to a Soviet form of Montezuma's revenge — the, ah, Trotskis — and the accommodations incredibly ordinary, even though the team stayed at the Intourist Hotel, highly rated by Soviet standards. Downtown and directly across from Red Square and the Kremlin, the place was much like a college dormitory.

The society itself was painfully slow moving, the people seldom in a hurry, the system slow to function. It was the absolute opposite of the fast-paced, fast-moving North American life, in style and substance. It was culture shock.

"I guess I got in trouble from the Russians," said Hull. "I got in trouble for something I said about Moscow. I said it looked like

Buffalo. I remember when I played in Buffalo later that season there was a big banner saying 'Go back to Moscow'.

"But the people in Moscow were wonderful. And most of the guys went to the things that were available (the famed Moscow circus and the Bolshoi ballet). We were able to enjoy it. We went to the theatre, and the museums. The Russians seem to be more into the arts than we are. There would be people lining up for miles to get into museums and things.

"The people would recognize us over there as the Canadian team. But they liked us. I think they were a little bored with the Russian style of hockey — they didn't realize hockey could be so exciting. At the Russian league games, if that was the NHL, there would be only 5,000 people going to the games. They had only ten or twelve shots on the net."

"It was a situation where we didn't understand the Russians," said Dionne. "We condemned them for a lot of things, for being different. It was political. They have their system, we have ours. There were a lot of aggravations and when you look at it now, it may have been childish. Of course, at the time, a lot of people were under intense pressure."

All the reviews, however, weren't quite so favourable. Phil Esposito, for one, admitted he was frightened the entire time he was in the Soviet Union. "I thought they would kill to win and that scared me," he said. "I didn't like it over there at all. I hated it. I'll never go back."

"It wasn't so bad," said Frank Mahovlich, who now operates a travel agency under his name in Toronto. "I guess you should experience things like that once."

But Mahovlich, interestingly, is alleged to have been involved in an incident that has become part of the grand lore of these Soviet excursions. According to Dick Beddoes, the tale goes that Mahovlich, suspicious that his room was bugged with listening devices, conducted a thorough search, which revealed an object neatly hidden beneath the rug. The carpet in the room was peeled back and sure enough there was some form of metal object, a listening device no doubt, attached to the floor. He then proceeded to unscrew it and kept unscrewing it until he was stopped by a loud crash from the floor below. A light fixture had dropped from the ceiling.

"He was psyched about Russia," said Serge Savard, Mahovlich's Canadien teammate. "We don't know what happened to him over there."

"I remember Frank said to Serge prior to the Vancouver game, 'You never know about the Russians. I bet at 3 a.m. they'll start up the jackhammers to try and keep us awake. We should take tents and camp away from Moscow,'" recalled Beddoes. "He was really bugged over there."

"Russia was tough," said winger Rod Gilbert. "It seemed like everyone — that referee (West German Joseph Kompalla), the hotel — was against us. The hotel facilities sucked. They stole our steaks and our beer. That's when we got mad — when they stole our beer after the fifth game. Okay, they could steal our steaks, but you steal beer from Canadian hockey players... Well, everyone was mad."

"There were about a hundred cases missing," said Park, "but what are you going to say?"

From humble origins comes motivation...

"When we got there, we had to wait in this bus for the

longest time," said Parise. "It was like they weren't expecting us. You know, right away the shit was starting. You don't invite someone to your house and leave them in the car for two hours.

"I remember on the flight from Toronto to Winnipeg, Cashman was talking to this Russian diplomat, and the diplomat was bragging about the Moscow airport and how great it was. You know, how wonderful the Russians were and all that bullshit. After a while, all that stuff started creating this great animosity."

This was the first time the Soviets had ever allowed a team and an entourage of this proportion, close to 3,000 people, into their country for a sporting series. Then, as now, they'll probably never be accused of being a tourist trap. But the presence of the spouses and the loyal fans seemed to rejuvenate a still somewhat despondent, though determined, Team Canada when it arrived. Spirits were lifted enough, anyway, that the events of the first day in Moscow, which could have been another devastating disruption, instead strengthened the resolve and drew the team even closer together.

At a morning workout, Sinden called the team to centre ice in the Luzhniki arena and announced the starting lineup for game five, the next night. It did not include Vic Hadfield, who took exception first at not playing, then at Sinden for not privately informing him.

Hadfield, discontented throughout, decided to call it a series and immediately asked Eagleson to arrange transportation home. Rick Martin and Jocelyn Guevremont, two youngsters, realized they didn't fit into the plans, either, and asked permission to return to their National Hockey League teams, the Buffalo Sabres and Vancouver Canucks respectively, figuring their time would be better spent preparing for the upcoming season. No hard feelings with them, and they first consulted with and received the blessings of Sinden.

"It wasn't an easy team to conduct," said Sinden. "They weren't getting paid, they didn't belong to any organization, they had come from other teams, given up their summers, and they weren't excited about being there. They didn't like it much in Moscow, the accommodations or anything.

"But I don't think the players, leaving affected us too much. They weren't going to play anyway, and some had been complaining all along. It started off like an all-star contest — everyone was going to get their ice time, everyone was going to play.

"We had promised everyone at least one game, but we found we had to go back on our word. That was the reality of it all. I was criticized for it by the players, but we had to win."

All three players returned home the next day, though before leaving they weren't treated kindly by the contingent of die-hard Canadian fans in Moscow, who had paid huge sums to be there, expected victory and weren't kind to any form of disruption. It seemed they doubted the defectors' sincerity and feared the already fragile confidence of the team might again be shattered.

"I remember we get over to Russia and we're having our first practice the day before the first game. It was a Thursday morning," said Eagleson, "and Vic skates over to the boards in the middle of practice and hollers at me 'Get me the hell out of here.' I talked to Harry and Fergie and I said if he wants to go, if any of them wants to go, then we'll get them out. There's no question at that point we had to get the team together, pull everyone together. We had been travelling with thirty-five players. It was too many, with fifteen guys sitting out every game."

At that point, the roster was reduced by four, since New York Islanders' young winger Bill Harris hadn't accompanied the team overseas. All agreed he wouldn't play and might as well attend training camp. As well, defenceman Serge Savard was still hobbled with a hairline fracture of his ankle, but while originally diagnosed as being finished for the series, it appeared he would play, likely in game six.

As for the defections, they were unsettling, but the team was so consumed with what lay ahead, they weren't the bother many expected.

"I think most guys realized they had careers to pursue," said Parise. "They had to get back to their own teams — the season was starting up soon. And with the series, if a guy didn't play, he didn't practise. When you're working on certain plays, you've got to use the guys who are going to play.

"So those guys weren't getting much ice time, and they had to get back to their own teams soon. I think they sort of felt, 'Hey, we're not going to play, anyway.' At that point you've got to take care of yourself.

"Some guys were offended. Gilbert Perreault (who departed after game five) was my roommate, and I know he's not a quitter. I think Hadfield sort of felt, 'Here's J.P. Parise playing and I'm not.' "

"I was rooming with Dale Tallon," recalled Rod Gilbert. "And that didn't work out so great, because he wasn't playing. And he was always saying, 'If you guys can't win, let me play,' or asking why he isn't playing. And I'm saying, 'Fuck, Dale, don't bother me,

I've got my own problems to worry about. Go talk to Bill White. Just don't bother me.' I wasn't mad at him — it was just so emotional. I didn't need that shit.

"Hadfield? I don't really know what it was that set him off. He was sort of caught in a catch-22. If he leaves, it looks bad. If he doesn't play, it looks bad. I think what upset him was the fact that in Sweden he was reunited with Jean Ratelle and me. Frank Mahovlich had stayed back in Canada (with a sore knee, but came to Moscow) and I guess Vic figured he was going to play. And then Mahovlich comes back, he hasn't skated in a week, and Sinden plays him instead of Vic.

"Oh, well, it's all fun and laughs now, but some of the reporters really gave it to him then. I felt bad for him."

"Hadfield really did get the brunt of it for leaving," agreed Park. "I was a teammate of Vic's and I understood his reasoning. He was a left winger and Frank Mahovlich had pulled something weird and stayed in Canada while we were in Sweden, and then he joined us in Moscow not having skated in a week. And Sinden decides to play him instead of Hadfield, who had been skating and practising all week.

"I was only twenty-four at the time, so I wasn't going to say anything to Sinden. But I did talk to Hadfield and I asked him not to leave, but that was his decision."

"I think that bothered him," said Ferguson of the decision to use Mahovlich ahead of Hadfield. "But on the big ice surface, we had to look at the skating aspect of it and Frank fit in."

"They took a lot of guys," said Hadfield, "so I realized we couldn't all play. It was just the way they did things. They treated us like we were ten or twelve years old. When we got to Russia,

Standing on guard...

◀ *Bobby Clarke was a tower of strength for Team Canada.*

▼ *Vic Hadfield takes up residence next to Vladislav Tretiak, the remarkable goalie.*

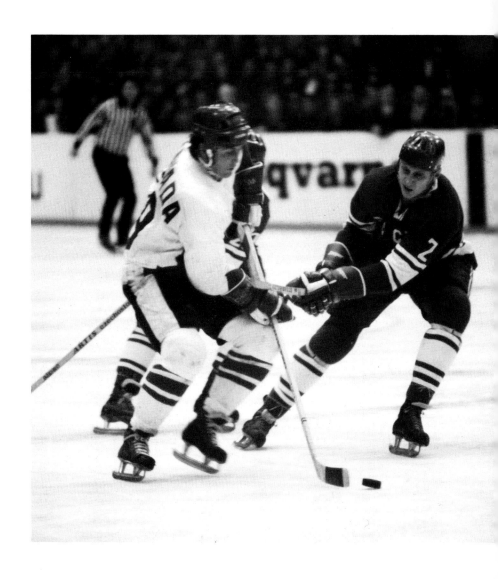

◀ *Paul Henderson on the attack again.*

▼ *Goalie Ken Dryden came up big when it mattered most.*

● ●

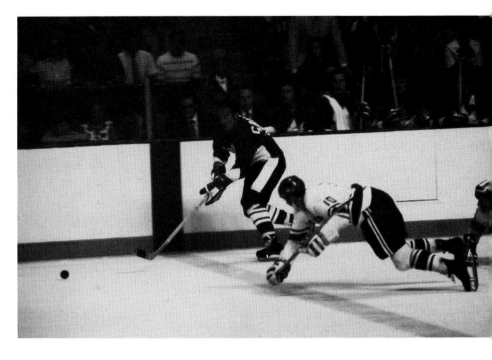

Frank Mahovlich, the Big M, leaves two Soviets down and out. ▲

Paul Henderson and Ron Ellis caused the Soviets fits. ▶

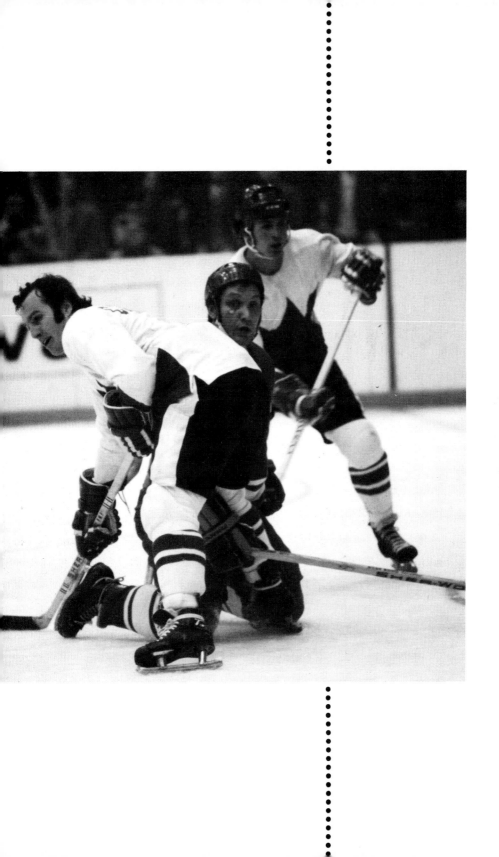

▲ *The colourless Luhzniki Arena in Moscow.*

▼ *The series was an emotional roller-coaster for Canadian hockey fans.*

▼Goalie Tony Esposito and defenceman Pat Stapleton attempt to hold the fort.

A toothless Bobby Clarke eludes the Soviets, including star winger Valeri ▲
Kharlamov.

• •

▼ *Paul Henderson and Vladislav Tretiak spent a lot of time together.*

▲ *The Big Red Machine on home ice.*

▼ *The thrill of victory...and the hero, Paul Henderson, in the middle of it all where he belonged.*

▲ *Canadian winger Rod Gilbert confirmed his status among the game's best players.*

Big left winger Alexander Yakushev proved to be among the very best in the world.

Phil Esposito (7) emerged as a leader, off and especially on the ice.

▼

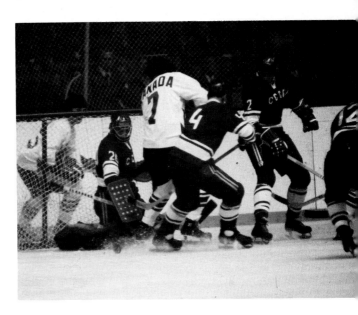

▼ *Celebrating another job well done.*

Phil Esposito emerges from the pack to salute the Canadian fans.

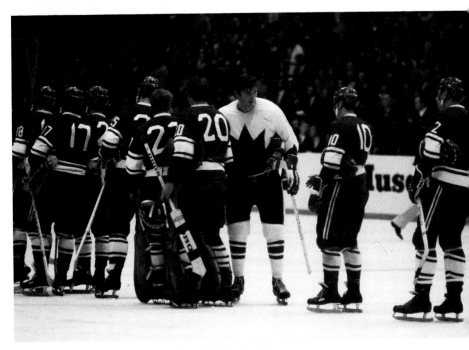

The series was glasnost a decade before its time.

they decided they were going to take seventeen or eighteen guys and play them for the rest of the series. The rest of the squad could stay and practise or go home. Eagleson told us we could go home.

"What bugged me is why didn't they notify the guys that weren't playing? They bring us all over there and we'd given up a lot of time, and they basically knew who was going to play, but they couldn't even tell us.

"A bunch of us had a meeting — guys like Perreault and Martin and Mikita were there, about fifteen guys. Most of us decided that we were going to go home. Then the next morning I get down to the bus and it's only Martin and Perreault. The other guys decided not to leave.

"I never did see eye to eye with the Eagle. Most of the guys who weren't playing weren't Eagle boys. The fact that I wasn't playing didn't bother me. It's just that they didn't have the balls to tell us.

"When I got back, I got support from guys around the league. I remember we played an exhibition game against Detroit, and Gordie Howe took me aside and gave me support for what I did. I don't really have any regrets. I was happy they ended up winning. I was cheering for them like everyone else."

Guevremont, meanwhile, lamented being called a deserter, but exited because his wife had fallen ill. That story, though, was not widely reported.

"When I was asked to play I got this letter that said we don't really want you, but we have no choice," said Guevremont. They had to take two guys from each team and I was the second guy from Vancouver. They stated quite clearly that I would never play in any game. But I wanted to go anyway just for the experience of practising with the best players in the world. I mean, I was only twenty-two, and I went to Russia.

"I came back because my wife was sick. We'd been there four days and she hadn't eaten anything. She had food poisoning or something. I didn't know the other three guys were coming back. We didn't get together or anything and decide. I guess I was just at the wrong place at the wrong time.

"After I decide to go, the next morning I get on the bus and there's Martin and Hadfield. When we got back to Montreal, the press was there. They started asking all these questions. I was asked how I felt being a deserter. That was a shock. It hurt. It was just too bad.

"I don't think the players ever forgave me for leaving. I suppose a few have, but there are some guys who've held a grudge. We weren't playing, we hadn't even practised with the team. The nonplaying guys couldn't practise. But I have no sore feelings. I knew somewhere along the line I'd get to tell my side of the story. I never regretted having to leave. I had to go with my wife."

Another who didn't play, but decided to stay, was Dionne, who also happened to be a client of Eagleson's.

"I wanted to leave, too," said Dionne. "I don't blame the other guys for leaving. Harry put the black aces in a position where they had no chance. They were ignored. All a player wants to know is if he has a chance of playing, but sometimes people are afraid to tell you because they're afraid they'll hurt your feelings.

"I remember one day I didn't go to practice. I slept in. I had had it. I know Punch Imlach was putting a lot of pressure on the Buffalo guys to go back. I was fortunate, though, to have a guy like the Eagle around, someone to talk to and figure out what was going on. It turned out to be exciting just to watch, even though there was no chance I was going to play."

Veteran goalie Eddie Johnston dressed for several games, but played just once, in one of the ill-fated exhibition games in Sweden. But he never contemplated leaving and had little sympathy for those who did.

"Myself, I was just happy to be picked for the series," he said. "Maybe at the time I didn't know how big an honour it was, but I was one happy guy. No question, for me it was a little easier than the others, maybe because the expectations of playing were always there and I did get a chance in a game in Sweden.

"For the guys not playing, well, they went over expecting to play, and next thing you know they're not part of the club. It was tough to accept for everyone. But we all felt they should've hung in until the end. It wasn't too much to ask. The team needed support, it didn't need any more problems. And the longer it went on, the closer you wanted to be. The thought of quitting never seriously crossed my mind."

And, as time would prove, the thought of quitting didn't cross the minds of the the remaining players, either.

CHAPTER SEVEN

The Omen

"**W**hen we got to Moscow," said defenceman Brad Park, "we had received at least 10,000 telegrams from the people back home wishing us good luck and stuff. So we taped all the telegrams to the walls in the dressing room so that every time we went to practice, or when we went out for a period, we would see all these telegrams. That was just great."

The outpouring of support from the fans in Canada was the composite result of several factors, including the residue of Phil Esposito's memorable speech in Vancouver, the three player defections, the presence of 2,700 fans in Moscow, and the Canadians' unwavering insistence on winning the series for themselves. The players, coaches and organizers had surmised they were on their own, the emotional ties of support back home severed. However, Team Canada had not been totally abandoned.

"Until what Espo said in Vancouver the people weren't exactly behind us, then bang, when we got over there we had walls upon walls of telegrams," commented centre Peter Mahovlich. "It wasn't until then, either, that we really started to realize we were playing for Canada."

"That speech by Phil really made the fans get behind us, no question," said winger Paul Henderson. "It was a very significant time, a significant factor in the series. It turned the fans around and everyone was saying, hey, let's get together here."

Surprisingly, by the time they departed Sweden in apparent shame and arrived in the Soviet Union, sentiment had swayed from anger to sympathy. People had realized the extent of the mission and a wave of backing had welled in Canada. And Team Canada needed it.

For the fifth game, head coach Harry Sinden continued to tinker and adjust, opting to come back with Tony Esposito in goal. He'd had a victory and a tie in two games in Canada and had been sharp in both outings. Defenceman Guy Lapointe was also available after a one-game absence because of injury, and he replaced Don Awrey. Sinden made three changes to his forward lines, inserting Jean Ratelle for Bill Goldsworthy, Peter Mahovlich for Dennis Hull, with J.P. Parise bumping the discontented Vic Hadfield from the lineup — and from the team.

The Soviets, meanwhile, made just two adjustments, both on defence, where Alexandr Gusev and Yuri Liapkin were both returned to the lineup. The pair had an offensive bent and the Soviets had not been getting contributions from the blue line — until this game.

Emotionally the Canadians were incredibly upbeat, considering in the past few days they had lost three teammates, defenceman Serge Savard was still nursing an ankle injury, they were thousands of miles away, in another time zone, a strange country, playing on an expanded ice surface with European officials, and faced with a staggering uphill battle.

"Even though we were behind," said winger Yvon Cournoyer, "the team still had a lot of confidence. It was amazing really, but we could see we were coming together. The trip to Sweden had helped. But we knew we had a group of guys who would stick together, and sometimes it's good to go on the road. Of course, going to Moscow is one helluva road trip."

With a crowd of sombre Soviet fans squeezed into the Luzhniki arena — a crowd that included three of the country's highest-ranking politicians, general secretary of the communist party Leonid Breshnev, president Nikolai Podgorny, and prime minister Alexei Kosygin — and 2,700 Canadian crazies assaulting the serenity, perhaps the first omen of what might follow was seen in the pre-game player introductions, usually an innocuous-enough time. But not on September 22, 1972.

Recalled manager Alan Eagleson, "Phil's name was called in the introductions, and as he stepped forward he stepped on a piece of a flower that was on the ice, fell and landed on his backside. But big Phil really played it up, got back up on one knee and gave that sweeping bow.

"I think that's when we started teaching the fans how to cheer. *Da, da,* Canada! *Nyet, nyet,* Soviet! We had trumpets playing, the Canadian fans were making all kinds of noise. And the Soviets didn't know what to make of it all. At that time, they didn't make too much noise — they still don't — except to whistle when they didn't like the officials' calls.

"I remember they came to take away the one kid who was playing the trumpet, but he would just pass it on to the next guy.

They would try to stop him and they would just keep passing it on. It was crazy."

"It wasn't until we got to Russia that we started to play well," said winger Rod Gilbert. "We were all playing like jazz. You know, improvising.

But when the music stopped, Team Canada's collective back would still be tightly pressed squarely to the wall, the possibility of defeat frightfully real. And more than just defeat, utter humiliation.

Team Canada started impressively in game five, checking with renewed vigour and dedication, much the way they had in the second game in Toronto, which, of course, was the only game they had won in the series. Their pestering of the Soviets again bothered the comrades, leading to mistakes, and ultimately goals.

At 15:30 of the opening period, the speedy Gil Perreault made another thrilling rush, this time deking wide on Gusev and setting up winger J.P. Parise in the slot. He easily beat goalie Vladislav Tretiak with a low shot, making Parise, who was regarded as somewhat of a surprise selection to the team, the first Canadian professional hockey player to score a goal in the Soviet Union.

"And that's one goal I will never forget," said Parise.

End of one period: Team Canada 1, Soviet Union 0.

"When we got to Moscow, we started to play better," said Peter Mahovlich. "We didn't think the refereeing was too good, but we were learning a lot of different things over there, like playing on the big ice surface, the sorts of penalties the referees call in international hockey. You can get away with some things we're used to, but not others.

"But we had adjusted pretty well and we were playing well in that game, too. Our checking was good and Tony was just excellent in goal. We got a lot of key saves from him."

Just 2:36 into the second period, hardnosed centre Bobby Clarke put the Canadians ahead 2-0, doing it with sheer hard work and determination. After winning a faceoff in the Soviet zone and pulling the draw back to Henderson, Clarke then manoeuvred into the slot, had a pass returned from Henderson, barged toward the goal and snuck a backhand shot between Tretiak's legs.

Midway through the period, Henderson tapped in Lapointe's rebound to put the Canadians ahead by three goals, and all seemed in order, although shortly after scoring, the Canadians received a mighty scare when Henderson crashed heavily, back first, into the boards and was briefly knocked unconscious, breaking up their most effective line. At the time, though, they were in complete control and Tony Esposito had stopped all twenty-two shots he'd faced, including a couple of really difficult saves late in the second period.

End of two periods: Team Canada 3, Soviet Union 0.

Having had two weeks between games, valuable time to refine their play and upgrade their conditioning, it appeared that Team Canada was at last beginning to come together on the ice, and the potential of the team was finally being realized. It was. And it wasn't.

Defensively, they had been playing well, and winger Ron Ellis had done a masterful job of shadowing and neutralizing the Soviets' dangerous winger, Valeri Kharlamov, keeping him scoreless.

"Everyone felt so strong about redeeming ourselves," said Sinden. "I think most of us were able to put the other things (defections, and so on) out of our minds. I remember we had really practised hard at the end of the week in Sweden, and we had two really intense workouts when we got to Moscow.

"You could see everyone was working hard. There was more intensity. We hadn't had that feeling since the first day of training camp. It really felt like we were finally a team. The emotion was finally there."

The emotion, though, would soon again take an unscheduled ride on the roller-coaster, crashing from the excitement of the first two periods to bitter disappointment in the end, for just when it seemed the Soviets were beaten, the unthinkable happened. During the final dozen minutes of the third period, the Canadians fell flat again.

The Soviets scored early, just 3:34 into the final period, when winger Yuri Blinov broke Esposito's shutout bid. But Team Canada didn't waver and less than two minutes later, Henderson, back from the infirmary, took a pass from Clarke and restored the three-goal bulge.

"I scored two goals in that sucker," said Henderson. "The second one put us ahead 4-1, but the Russians just kept coming back and coming back, and we couldn't stop them."

In the shocking span of just five and a half minutes, the Soviets miraculously produced four goals to assume a 5-4 lead they would protect to victory. The comeback began at 9:05, with Viacheslav Anisin redirecting Liapkin's pass behind Esposito. Eight seconds later, Vladimir Shadrin completed a nifty three-way passing play with a goal. And at 11:41, Gusev tied it, beating Esposito with a high shot.

"When they came back," said Cournoyer, "it didn't shock us the way it did in the first game, or any of the other games. We knew it was possible. We tried not to fall back into a defensive shell, but I guess we did and we were angry that it did happen."

Finally, at 14:46, Vladimir Vikulov produced the winning goal, taking advantage of a slight mixup at the Canadian blue line, stealing a drop pass from Clarke intended for defenceman Rod Seiling. Five goals on 11 shots and a 5-4 lead.

"I sure let the team down in that one," recalled Tony Esposito. "I had played pretty well the first two periods, then all of a sudden I couldn't stop anything. They really came at us hard, but we should never have lost it."

"I remember Tony came to me afterwards and said he let the team down in that game," said Eagleson. "But the guy had played so well for us throughout. It wasn't his fault. And nobody got down afterwards."

Team Canada valiantly tried to at least tie it, but then Tretiak assumed the role of hero and stopper, first frustrating big Frank Mahovlich on a breakaway and arranging another on Cournoyer late in the game.

"We thought we had learned our lesson in Montreal when we were ahead 2-0 early and lost," said backup goalie Eddie Johnston, "but it happened again. Maybe we got too anxious, trying to pour it on. But we got caught, whatever it was, by their great transition game. They could go from defence to offence so quickly, and it caused us big problems. To put it bluntly, we really got burned."

Final score: Soviet Union 5, Team Canada 4.

Suddenly, and perhaps inconceivably, Team Canada found itself in an even more desperate predicament, requiring victories in the final three games, all on Moscow ice, to win the series. Interestingly, though, as they left the ice that day, shocked and dejected and angry, they were also given a rousing standing ovation by the gathering of Canadian fans, virtually remembered now as the symbol of their defiance.

"One reason this series was so special," said Henderson, "is because we never gave up. Never did anyone say after that game, 'Well, that's it, we're done.' We always had that feeling we were going to win. It sounds strange, but I never felt we were going to lose the series, not even after that game."

While in an obviously tenuous situation in terms of the series standings, no longer a margin for error, the team had a much better feeling about itself and its chances. As Henderson put it, losing had never fit into the equation, and they were convinced they would beat the Soviets.

"I was proud of how we played in that game," said Phil Esposito. "I said after the game we weren't going to lose again. I was convinced of it. And I'm sure if we played another ten games we wouldn't have lost any of them, either. They just couldn't match our emotion, and we were starting to come together as a team on the ice."

"We did look like a pretty good team that game," agreed Sinden. "We knew we could beat them from the game back in Toronto, and this effort proved to us that that game wasn't just a reaction to getting pounded in the opening game. We hadn't completely arrived, but the emotion was there and I felt as good as you can ever feel after losing a game."

In addition to losing the game, though, the list of Team Canada's dearly departed swelled by one. Perreault became the fourth man out in just two days when he asked permission to return home and join the Buffalo Sabres' training camp.

Curiously, Perreault had played the past two series games, in Vancouver and the opener in Moscow, and played well, if not often. At the time, he insisted he wasn't in condition, didn't think he fit into the plans, and figured he might as well leave, too. Perreault's timing in stepping out of his appointed place in history, though, was horrible, with the Canadians in a must-sweep situation.

"He had played a couple of great games for us, scored a great goal," said Eagleson, "but he left, too. We just couldn't afford to have those guys around, because the team was just starting to pull together."

"It wasn't like I walked out on them," said Perreault. "That's just what a lot of (media) guys said. I talked it over with Harry before I left. I wasn't upset or mad. It was just that I wasn't going to be playing much anyway and I wanted to get ready to play with the Sabres.

"I remember thinking at the time that I would get other chances to play in a series like that one. I was still young and I knew that my time was still ahead of me. I was very proud of those guys for what they did, but I have never regretted what I did."

The defection of Perreault, though, was not as disturbing as the three that had occurred a day earlier. The team had discovered a confidence in itself in game five and a focus. It would not be easily broken.

"That loss should've been demoralizing for everyone," said Eagleson. "But instead, the 3,000 fans we had over there gave us a standing ovation after the game. That was a key factor, too. I didn't know until after that first game in Moscow just what was happening in Canada, either, what impact the series had.

"And even though we lost that game, that was the first time the players really came together as a team. I remember afterwards I went in the dressing room and guys were jumping up and down ready to play."

"I don't think anybody except the team believed we could win the series at that point," said Cournoyer. "It was an awfully tall order, but we really did believe we would do it."

CHAPTER EIGHT

Holy Moses

"We were depressed after losing that fifth game," recalled winger Rod Gilbert. "But everyone remained very professional about it. Sure there were some guys who were getting down, the guys who hadn't been playing. But we stuck together. We knew we had to win each game after that and we were there to kick some ass."

It's a hoary cliché in the lexicon of sports, but for Team Canada there was no tomorrow. A loss in game six, or seven, or eight, and the international hockey bragging rights would belong to the Soviets, who had a veritable stranglehold on the series, leading 3-1-1.

"After the first four games in Canada we were certain we could beat the Canadians in Moscow," said Soviet centre Boris Mikhailov. "The victory in the first game in Montreal had brought the Canadian team down. It was — how do you say? — a big upset. We knew the Canadian pros were at the same level as us and we were very confident of our chances. We had no doubts.

"After the first game at home, game five, we came back to

win and we were all very certain we would win the series then. Maybe the team had become overconfident."

The Canadians were quite aware, too, of the lasting effects of defeat, the eternal embarrassment, and that they would return home shamed in the eyes of a nation that had suddenly rallied to lend emotional support from afar. That is what they call pressure. But if the Soviets had figured all angles on the ice, they hadn't given sufficient respect to the intangibles of sports — pride and determination. Team Canada had become an emotional team, driven together by adversity, and their emotion would become a significant factor. At times, it was the only edge they possessed. In essence they were together in spirit because they felt so damn alone at the summit.

"The fifth game, even though we lost, actually gave us more of a sense of professionalism," continued Gilbert. "I mean, we're not winning but we're doing our job. And all the reporters are writing how we're screwing up. Well, the reporters aren't on the ice. So we just said, well, fuck the reporters. I mean, I'm going to miss the net just to piss off a reporter?

"But in those final games, we just concentrated on playing hockey. We had found their weaknesses. We played differently. We finally had more information about them. Any time you play a team five, six times, you're going to have more information. So we discussed weaknesses with our teammates and had a much better feeling.

"It was about the sixth game that we started to feel as though we were in good physical shape. After that fifth game we were very close, too. We felt we could overcome. We knew we were going to win. I just sensed it."

But first there were more hurdles to overcome, some expected, some not. The Soviets were at home and ahead, confident playing on the big ice surface, and they were playing with European officials in control, the same pair — Franz Baader and Joseph Kompalla (or Baader and Worse as Alan Eagleson called them) — who had officiated the two debacles in Sweden a week earlier.

And there was the pressure, which has curious effects on both individuals and teams. More than anything else, perhaps, it offers the truest indication of the depth and character and resolve of players and their team.

"Well, maybe if we had started over in Moscow," said defenceman Don Awrey, "the Russians wouldn't have taken the early lead. Maybe the pressure would have gotten to them. You certainly felt the responsibility of playing for your country."

A factor Team Canada seemingly had in its favour was experience, not with any summit series, but with playing in the intense, pressure-filled National Hockey League playoffs. They were at least equipped to deal with the attendant spiritual lows.

"We couldn't afford to lose, we all knew that, and the pressure really was unbelievable," said winger Yvon Cournoyer. "But we were confident. I know with the Montreal Canadiens, and other players had been through it with other teams, we had our backs to the wall a lot of times, but with a little luck and a lot of hard work you can come out of it. I think the fact we had that experience in those situations really helped us. It made us confident."

"It was a case of us all having to suck it up and we all knew it," said Eddie Johnston. "Everything was there in front of us. But we also knew we could beat this team, even in Russia. We just had to eliminate the lapses. Play it smart."

Heading into the sixth game, the off-ice troubles of the team had all been resolved, or at least quieted. The troika of Vic Hadfield, Richard Martin and Jocelyn Guevremont had departed before the fifth game, and afterward, young centre Gilbert Perreault had requested to leave, a decision that was something of a shocker, considering he had played the previous two games and played well, producing a goal and an assist.

"The defections..." began co-coach John Ferguson. "I don't think the players were realistic about them. I mean, things can change overnight with injuries and stuff. The funny thing is, Harry and I had talked and we figured on putting Hadfield in the sixth game, then he decides to leave before the fifth game. But I don't think the defections bothered the players."

According to one report of the day, Hadfield's lawyer at the time, player agent Bob Woolf, had travelled to Moscow, heard his player was expected to dress for the sixth game and immediately began phoning home, but soon discovered the inherent inefficiencies of the Soviet telephone system. He never did get in contact with his client.

"That's bullshit," countered Hadfield, on the subject of his being slated for the sixth game. "I got along with John Ferguson, and he did a good job keeping the guys motivated and stuff, but I think that was to make them look better for my leaving."

"We had the guys leave and all," said winger Dennis Hull, "and Hadfield really took the brunt of it, but he just wanted to play. He just wanted a chance. I wanted the chance just like Vic and the rest. I think they made a serious mistake deciding to go home. It looked like they were leaving a sinking ship, but I can understand how Vic felt. He was a fifty-goal scorer and just wanted the chance to play.

"I was fortunate, actually, because with Hadfield gone and Frank Mahovlich hurting, they were short of left wingers, so I got inserted with two great players, Ratelle and Gilbert. I'm just fortunate after all these years to have played and it's something I'll never forget."

Harry Sinden made four lineup changes for the sixth game, beginning with replacing Tony Esposito in goal with the winless Ken Dryden. Given Dryden's track record against the Soviets, in this series and in the 1969 world championships, the move raised a few eyebrows. Tony Esposito had faltered in the third period of the fifth game, but generally had played well throughout the series. They wouldn't have been in the position for a comeback without him.

"I was quite certain," said Dryden, "when we left Sweden or arrived in Moscow, I can't recall, that I wouldn't be playing. In Sweden they had used Tony Esposito and Eddie Johnston and both had played well. I thought I was basically done, but I said to myself what I had to do was keep at it, if nothing else the season would be beginning when we returned and I could use the practice time.

"After those two losses (game one and game four) and with Eddie Johnston playing well in Sweden, I didn't think I'd play again. At the time I was told, I think it was by Fergie, that I would play the sixth game, Tony would play the seventh, and I'd play the eighth. It was all set out before the sixth game. Just recently, I had the first chance to see the games themselves, not just the highlights. I had always avoided watching them. In the summer of 1973 the CBC ran a game a week, and I can remember thinking when it happened that this was terrific. I've gone through these games one way and missed so much of what went on. But here's a chance to sit back and enjoy the games, knowing how they end.

"I watched the first five minutes and left the room. I couldn't watch — the feelings were far too close. I knew what had happened, but it didn't matter. It was too hard to watch.

"I finally watched the games this year because I had to watch (as part of research for a television series and accompanying book). It was a lot easier to watch, too. The first game was awful to watch and parts of others, but the games in Moscow went a lot better than I remembered. But I was so wrapped up in everything, I almost have no impression of how I played."

The other key change involved steady defenceman Serge Savard, who would never lose a game to the Soviets in his entire career, returned from an ankle injury, one that was supposed to have shelved him from the series. Savard bumped Rod Seiling from the roster.

"The ten days in Sweden and the extra practice days really helped me," said Savard. "I wasn't sure if I could play, but I started skating again. I wasn't one hundred percent for that game, but I was getting better."

"He was our best defenceman," said Clarke. "When we got him back for the sixth game, that really seemed to settle things down. He's a big man who could play thirty minutes a game, slow it down when we needed it, pick up the pace when we had to. We had a good feeling when he was in the lineup."

Up front, Hull and Berenson assumed the positions of Perreault and Frank Mahovlich.

"By that time," remembered Berenson, playing just his second game, "we could keep up. We picked up the pace. They had really trained for this, and we were just getting into shape. That first game, we were coming off the ice gasping for breath, wondering how we were going to keep up with them. They could really skate. But by the sixth game, the pace of the game on the ice seemed slower, because we were catching up.

"I think the fifth game was the turning point. We were leading — we should have been destroyed losing that game — but in the locker room we were really excited. We really could beat this team. We had outplayed them and outscored them and then we let it slip away. In that (the sixth) game, I just wanted to help the team. It's tough to step in and play, and I was a little bit out of synch most of the game.

"Harry was in a no-win situation with the players, unless the team won. He couldn't satisfy everyone, and Fergie kept the players loose and motivated. There were a lot of big egos on that team. Sinden had to walk a bit of a tightrope. I don't think he made many friends over there."

"We had pretty much settled on one lineup," said Sinden. "Maybe one or two changes, but we needed that continuity. It really seemed to help. And we had decided we were going to use both goalies throughout because of the pressure that was involved."

The Soviets, sensing victory themselves, made five roster changes, two on defence, three up front, none of them major, as they continued to move all their players in and out of the lineup.

They were in it for the experience, they said. And never blushed saying so.

Prior to the game, the Canadians received more telegrams from fans in Canada, something they now remember as lifting their spirits even further. They suddenly didn't feel quite so alone in their pursuit of vindication.

"There were something like 1,000 telegrams from Prince Rupert to the Northwest Territories and they were all saying, 'Good Luck, Canada,'" said Eagleson. "In the runway outside the dressing room, we had them all plastered to the walls and we circled the hometowns of the players. It made for a real Canadian feeling. Then we started getting phone calls from back home at all hours of the day. It was an amazing thing."

"The telegrams and those 3,000 fans that came over to Russia with us was just great," said winger J.P. Parise. "What great support. The fans were all in the same end of the rink, all this red, white and yellow. It was something compared to the Russian spectators, who were all in grey suits and wouldn't show any emotion.

"There was so much electricity in the air. We had a feeling that nothing would detract us from our focus. Nothing would deter us. After that first game in Russia, the way we played, it was obvious our conditioning was so much better. Before, we were out of shape, there was no time to handle the puck. But now, because we were in better shape, the game had started to slow down for us. We were starting to have control.

"You know, we scored some shit goals and we said, 'Hey, guys, now we can play.' You know, it was the first time a lot of us had played the criss-cross. We weren't used to the weaving around the ice, but we grew into that. After the fifth game, we said, 'We've arrived.' "

Adjustments were a significant factor in the outcome of the series, too. The Soviets had discovered a way to play the Canadians, found success, and stubbornly adhered to it. But the Canadians were always adjusting, adapting, experimenting with new things and finding new successes in breaking the Soviets' mastery early in the series. If there has been a major change to the Soviet game since, it has been in their newfound willingness to change.

The most notable changes arrived in the sixth game. For instance, Team Canada was now able to break up the Soviets' intricate passing plays, they were able to skate with them and interrupt their criss-crossing in the neutral zone. And they were back to bumping, backchecking with determination, and holding the blue line.

"Sinden, to me, was way ahead of his time," said Parise. "He had all the info in his head, from scouts and things like that. There wasn't any video then, and he could see something on the ice and then in between periods figure out a way to play against it. What a picture he had from the whole thing.

"When you're coaching, you can't always watch the game. But Sinden could do that, still know what was going on and adjust. (New York Islanders') Al Arbour has that ability, too. I had played for Sinden, so I knew him. We started our minor-league careers together, so we understood each other. Sinden has the great picture. He was able to see the strong points and the weak points of the Russians."

"I didn't think we adjusted that much during the games," said defenceman Bill White. "We tried to stand them up at the blue line, but that's fundamental defence. Keep the play outside the blue line instead of letting them come in three abreast and do the drop passes and stuff."

Hull, though, disagrees and believes the difference in coaching philosophies was ultimately a deciding factor.

"You had to admire the skills the Russians had," said Hull. "Guys like Yakushev and Kharlamov were two of the best players in the world. I think if they had been allowed by the coaches to play our style, they would have won. But they didn't adapt. They played the same way from the first minute to the last minute.

"Take Pat Stapleton and Bill White. You know, everyone talks about defencemen as individuals — like Bobby Orr, Raymond Bourque, Paul Coffey — as being great defencemen. But Bill White and Pat Stapleton were one of the best defensive pairings ever to play. They complemented each other so well.

"Those two guys would amaze the Russians. They were always trying to pass up the centre. Well, White and Stapleton learned to move up and intercept the pass at centre. But the Russians would continue to do it. They wouldn't change their game plan.

"And the goaltender, Tretiak, instead of coming out to cut off the angle, he would always stay in the net. They just wouldn't change."

Sinden and Ferguson also managed to create a sharper focus for the team, begging them not to concern themselves with the fact they had to win the three games ahead. Instead, worry about the one period confronting them.

"Take it one step at a time," said defenceman Brad Park.

"The fifth game was the biggest downer because we were up and lost it. The day after, we just started talking about taking it one game at a time, one period at a time. We couldn't start looking two, three games down the road. And Sinden was always telling us, 'One game at a time, one period at a time.' Everyone knew we had to win the final three games, but we didn't think about it."

"We obviously had to bear down in the sixth game," said Ferguson. "We changed the lineup again. I think players in that situation are looking for guidance, looking for anything we might have on the opposition, but there weren't a lot of between-period or pre-game speeches. We knew what we had to do. We had some leaders on that team. Bobby Clarke was one. Phil Esposito certainly was one. And Serge Savard when he played."

The other change for this game was the attitude and approach of the players. They had renewed confidence in themselves, and proper respect for the Soviets.

"Until they showed respect for their opposition they were going nowhere," said international hockey expert Billy Harris, a former coach and player. "But they finally realized what they were up against, and got stronger as the games went on. They realized they had to play at the top of their game to win. It's amazing what they were able to accomplish in Moscow."

A group of Canadian fans managed a great feat of their own when it was discovered before the sixth game that now fewer than a thousand of them weren't going to get their tickets for the game, another apparent mixup in the Soviet system. Several efforts to appease them were disregarded, but they were ultimately provided with the tickets they had originally purchased. Slow but sure. That's how the Soviet system works.

"The bullshit over there was incredible," said winger Wayne Cashman.

The, um, hijinks would soon carry over onto the ice in the form of officials Kompalla and Baader, who confounded the Canadians with their penalty calls and apparent missed offsides. Remember, back then in international hockey there were only two officials, not the two linesmen and a referee used in the NHL. The two men are both empowered to call penalties, and both must work the lines calling offsides. And neither did a very good job of it. But the two-man system, using Europeans, was one of the concessions made in April, 1972, during final negotiations to entice the Soviets to play.

In the first period, which ended without any goals, the Canadians were given all three minor penalties, including a double-minor to centre Phil Esposito, but they neatly killed them. The team, though, was beginning a slow boil.

"The officiating was just incredible," said Hull.

"It was the worst I had ever seen," said Sinden.

Just 1:12 into the second period, the Soviets opened the scoring when defenceman Yuri Liapkin beat Dryden with a low shot from the blue line. But the Canadians' confidence never wavered. They were playing well and thoroughly dominated the next few minutes, briefly stunning the Soviets with three goals in the space of just one minute and twenty-three seconds.

Hull tied it at 5:13, flipping a rebound over Tretiak, after Gilbert had taken advantage of a rare Soviet giveaway. At 6:31, Berenson gained possession behind the Soviet net and centred to Cournoyer in the slot. Fifteen seconds later, Paul Henderson intercepted a pass at centre by a visibly unsettled

Soviet defence and beat Tretiak with a hard slapshot from high in the slot.

It was 3-1, but the officials — Baader and Worse — were just beginning to get involved, to affect the precise order of proceedings. They began by issuing coincidental minor penalties to Guy Lapointe and Valeri Vasiliev, followed with a phantom slashing call to Clarke and a ten-minute misconduct when he argued it. Later still, Hull was sent off, and nine seconds into his penalty, big winger Alexandr Yakushev sliced the Canadians' lead to one goal, beating Dryden from in close.

The worst, though, was still to come. Phil Esposito had collided with burly Soviet defenceman Alexandr Ragulin, was knocked down again by the comrade, but wound up being given a five-minute major for high-sticking when, during the scuffle, his stick flew up and accidentally opened a small cut on Ragulin's chin. Further complaining from the bench brought another minor penalty. So, with their lead suddenly tenuous, the momentum swaying, the Canadians were two men short for the conclusion of the period and the opening of the third.

"That refereeing sure woke the players up to what they were up against," said Cashman. "I mean, this Russian team were qualified as professionals. To them, it was a dead-serious thing. It was really a bullshit propaganda plot and it turned a lot of the players off."

"The refereeing was beyond belief," said Hull. "You wouldn't believe it. They're very nationalistic about their calls. It's like that call in the world junior championships (Anchorage, Alaska, 1989) when the referee said the Canadian had knocked the puck in with his hand. Well, that was a beautiful play. His hand was nowhere near the puck. But it's almost like the referee is waiting for a chance to make a call like that. He's thinking ahead of the situation.

"It's the totally opposite over here (in Canada) when we play the Russians. Our refs bend over backwards to show that they're not playing favourites. It's so upsetting when the refereeing is bad like it was over there. When you're used to the NHL, where it's so perfectly fair, then you get a penalty called just because the Russians are losing, you just have to put up with it, I guess, but it's frustrating. You wind up spending half the game killing penalties."

Between periods, the Canadians were a confused and angry hockey team. But they were also winning, though that was far from mind, and the coaching staff knew it had to cool the guys down emotionally, soothe the tempers, yet maintain their strong resolve.

"I remember after the second period, Harry and I went in and really gave it to them. We thought we had blown it," said Ferguson. "But you also try to dwell on the positives, and just remind them of the negatives. We knew all the good Soviet players, so we would tell them to check Yakushev a little closer, or stay near Kharlamov and stay away from penalties."

Outside the dressing room, though, Ferguson was enraged by the incompetent officiating. "The business with the referees really stirred us up," said Sinden. "Fergie threatened not to let us play, even though he wasn't in charge. But Fergie could pull that off."

The Canadians were tardy returning to the ice, inspiring speculation they were protesting the officials' work and pulling out. They were supremely bugged, but Sinden merely wanted some extra time to calm his players.

"Plus, there was all kinds of water on the ice and we didn't want to go back out until it had frozen," said Sinden.

A combination of stellar penalty killing by the likes of Park, Peter Mahovlich, Savard and Berenson, veteran defenceman Gary Bergman, and excellent work by Dryden in goal allowed them to preserve their lead. They also had a stroke of good fortune, late in the second period. The Soviets scored a goal that almost no one noticed — including the officials.

"The game should've been tied," said Eagleson, "but they've got that net that hangs down in the goal to keep the puck in. Well, it kept this one out. We were shorthanded at the time and Kharlamov flipped in a shot, and the puck went four or five inches behind Dryden. But he caught the puck off the net and pulled it out. No goal."

Dispatches of the day described the shot as going off the goalpost, Kharlamov a little too nonchalant with his shot, standing alone in front of Dryden, whose vindication would ultimately reflect that of the team.

"The Soviets like to make the goal-mouth pass and hit the defenceman sneaking down to the net, or hit someone else a few feet off the corner," recalled Dryden. "The pass came over to my right, the left-wing side, close to the net. We all moved for the shot, and the pass was made back to the other side, to Kharlamov.

"He shot and had the whole open net, but his shot hit my pads on such an angle that the puck headed toward the goal post and the mesh inside. The puck hit there and I'll get back to where *there* is. But the rebound came right back into my glove.

"It was the sort of thing that no one could quite believe — the goal judge, the referee, Kharlamov. I'm still not honestly sure if the puck hit the post or the mesh. But the whole series of events were so improbable, no one was certain enough to celebrate or to argue that it went in."

"I don't like to say this," said defenceman Don Awrey, "but Dryden never really played that well in international competition, and I'm sure it was the pressure of representing your country. He could play phenomenal in the Stanley Cup, but it's different when you're playing for your country. And you have to have great goaltending to win a series like that."

Dryden, though, improved immensely after shaky efforts in the opener in Montreal and game four in Vancouver. He was outstanding in this game, and would return for game eight.

Before the issue was settled in game six, though, the Canadians bravely holding their 3-2 lead, the officials would make for a tense finish, giving a questionable penalty to Ron Ellis at 17:39. On that night, Team Canada received thirty-one minutes in penalties, many, but not all, deserved; the Soviets received just four. But the Canadians did not break in the final minutes; they held their lead, and afterwards were assured the officials would not return in the series. Or so they thought.

"I remember after the game, Dale Tallon (a Team Canada reserve) and I waited at the exit for the referees to come off the ice," recalled Bobby Orr, whose knee injury kept him from playing but didn't keep him from accompanying the team throughout the series. "We were both shaking we were so upset, and they were shaking, too, but for a different reason. We yelled at those guys like a couple of fools, but that's how emotional it was."

Team Canada was able to console itself with its impressive victory, of course, but a huge emotional toll had been exacted, tapped by the frustration of the officials' work, by the pressure of the task at hand, by the relentless play of the Soviets.

"It was a dramatic win, that's for sure," said Johnston. "It was a sign of what was to follow, I suppose. We knew if we could get ahead in a game again, we could shut them down. The problem was we were coming from behind all the time."

Interestingly, the winning goal, which was scored early in the second period, was produced by Henderson, who would have been credited with scoring the winning goal in the fifth game had the Canadians hung on. He would, of course, proceed to produce big goals in the final two games, too.

"I didn't think anything special was happening to me, though," said Henderson. "I just felt part of a team that was going to win."

"There was one funny thing about the sixth game," said Hull. "Before we went out for the second period, I had just been inserted into the lineup for that game, and Paul Henderson comes up to me and says, 'You're the new guy. You have to be our Moses and lead us.' Well, Henderson turned out to be our Moses."

CHAPTER NINE

Night Games

"After the sixth game I said we would win the series, the Russians couldn't beat us," recalled backup goalie Ed Johnston, who had not left the bench but for one exhibition game in Sweden. "I sounded like a prophet afterwards, but at the time it was probably more a case of trying to keep the guy's spirits up, keep the boys believing.

"Maybe after winning that fifth game, the Russians thought they could clinch the series, but we took a bit of the starch out of them and we shut them down. We always knew we could open it up, but being able to shut them down, that was really very important. And we did it. On the big ice. That had to bug them a lot.

"At that point, we were in better shape, and getting adjusted. We were coming together. We had a very good feeling about ourselves and that win in the sixth game really made us believe. Thankfully, it wasn't too late."

"After we won the sixth game, I just knew it was downhill for the Russians from there," said winger Rod Gilbert. "I knew we would win it."

The fun — and games — however, were just beginning. Off the ice. The Soviet authorities have long had a reputation for playing head games with their opposition, especially when they get them inside the borders of the vast Soviet Union. They're psychological ploys, little needless bothers and nuisances that keep building up to the point where they can — and inevitably do — irritate and unsettle a team. Once Team Canada won the sixth game, the mind games began, and it didn't take much to stir the already vivid imaginations of the players, whose knowledge of the Soviet Union and its people was sorely limited. But then, the Soviet Union was much more the great beyond back then, and Team Canada was the first pro hockey team to visit. There was an attendant fear of the Soviets, who were known more for spy rings and the KGB than they were for their hockey abilities.

"When we finally won over there, it started," said organizer Alan Eagleson. "And when we finally got even with the Russians in the seventh game, well, the last forty-eight hours were absolutely sinful.

"The first thing the Russians did was before the seventh game. We had a practice scheduled for ten in the morning and when we got to the rink there had to be 500 kids on the ice. The Russians told us we had to go out to another rink to practise. I told them, 'No fucking way.' So I just sent Rod Gilbert and Dennis Hull out on the ice and told them to start shooting some pucks. Within ten seconds the ice was clear."

"We were reacting to our rights," recalled Gilbert. "We didn't hit anybody, we just chased them off the ice, that's all. We were very emotional at that time. We had lost all three games in Canada, we had lost the first game over there and then finally won. We were ready to play. And then all this bullshit about stealing our beer and having the practice time changed happens. They said we were late. That was bullshit."

If there was one thing that bothered the Canadians almost as much as losing and the criticisms they were forced to endure, it was the Soviets' off-ice hijinks, some seemingly intentional, others simply a product of an everyday society that isn't as advanced as North America's. What they regard as luxuries are what we regard as necessities, so those things aren't priorities in the Soviet Union. But there were other mysterious happenings that served to distract the players.

"They just tried to get us pissed off all the time," said coach Harry Sinden. "They're masters at all that kind of stuff. We didn't make issues out of those things, though, but we let it be known through the grapevine that we were having a lot of trouble with them, with the administrative things, the referees and the practices. They don't like that."

There were things that went bump in the night, too. They ranged from telephone calls in the middle of the night, with no voice at the other end, to intercoms that would turn on without help, little voices...

"I was staying with my wife," said defenceman Brad Park. "They had intercoms in the rooms and they would come on in the middle of the night even though you had turned them off. And the phone would ring in the middle of the night. You would get up and pick it up, and there would be no one on the other end.

"I wasn't scared, though. Heck, the whole world was paying attention to this series, so they weren't going to do anything to you with the whole world watching."

A result of some of the subtle mind bending was that the Canadian players began imagining things were going on, that they were being followed and purposely bothered, sometimes when nothing was happening.

"We would get a lot of calls in the middle of the night," said winger Paul Henderson. "There were a lot of inconveniences, they played the mind games, but I guess to a degree we were willing to believe a lot of things that weren't going on, too."

"We were getting phone calls every fucking night," countered Phil Esposito, whose disdain for the Soviet Union is well documented. "It was driving me nuts. You always had the feeling you were being watched. And there's no doubt in my mind we were being watched. It was fucking crazy over there. I hated it."

Nevertheless, the little bothers and inconveniences essentially became another motivating force for Team Canada, strengthening their determination to beat the Soviets. The series had long since evolved into something more than a hockey series. It had become a political battle, a war, a confrontation of systems and beliefs. And the angrier the players got, the more determined they became to prove their system, country and talents to be best.

"We kept hearing how great the Russians were and all that crap," said winger J.P. Parise. "It became a hatred and we just wanted to beat those bastards. We were going to do anything to win, and show everybody that we were the best.

"Being in Russia sort of did it. Nobody needed any added motivation, but if we had to stay in Canada for those games it might have been different. But in Russia, with the early wake-up calls, and them stealing our beer... After practice we would be visiting a little bit, and there would be guys following us all the time. KGB were following us! I mean, Christ! The common people were really nice, they treated us well.

"But it was just so weird in Russia. I mean, the team told us not to play cards, because you can't leave the country with more money than you came in with. You had to declare all this stuff. But a lot of things that happened really gave us some extra motivation, there's no question."

Stealing a Canadian's beer abroad is a definite no-no, akin to a glove in the snout, a heartbreaking loss, guaranteed to anger and produce regrettable consequences. Revenge. Almost every Canadian remembers, too, the cases of beer disappearing after they had cleared through the excruciatingly thorough Soviet customs officers at the airport.

"We had brought a lot of food over, but we lost a lot of our steaks, too," said Johnston. "They never made it through customs. They probably couldn't believe what they were seeing. To be over there was culture shock for all of us. We were pretty well restricted as to what we could do or see, but from what we saw it sure made you appreciate Canada a whole lot more. It was an unforgettable experience, that's for sure. I remember when we got back, just sinking my teeth into a hotdog, or a hamburger, felt like winning the lottery."

"You hear it's bad over there, but you don't know how bad until you get there," said Yvon Cournoyer. "People still say it's bad, so you can imagine what it was like seventeen years ago. But we were there to play hockey, and it made everyone appreciate a little bit more what we had at home. I didn't mind just having to play there, but I certainly wouldn't go back over on a vacation."

This trip, however, was all business. Serious business.

If there was a blessing to begin the seventh game, it was that the two West German officials, Joseph Kompalla and Franz Baader, were not present, replaced by Rudolph Bata and Uve Dahlberg, who were better, but only slightly.

Sinden made a couple of changes to the lineup, continuing with his endless — though now successful — tinkering. He replaced centre Red Berenson with winger Bill Goldsworthy, and maintained his goaltending rotation, coming back with Tony Esposito in place of Ken Dryden.

"After the sixth game, I sat down for dinner with Harry and Fergie and said, 'What about the goaltending situation?'" said Eagleson. "They said, 'We're going with Tony — we need two goalies to win this thing.' I couldn't figure out what they were going to do next with the goalies, but they knew what they were doing. It worked out."

The Soviets were without fleet forward Valeri Kharlamov for the seventh game. He had succumbed to a sore and badly bruised ankle, believed to have been the result in the previous game of a Bobby Clarke slash, an incident widely reported and condemned by the Soviet press.

"Clarke was really starting to mature as a player in that series," remembered assistant coach John Ferguson. "You know, the thing about Clarke is you didn't have to wind him up to play. I remember Kharlamov, his ankle was hurting pretty bad, and I mentioned to Clarke that his ankle was hurting, so Clarke went out and gave him a little tap. Oh, yeah, he got the message loud and clear."

"Kharlamov had been eating them up," said journalist Dick Beddoes. "Clarke told me the story back at the reunion. It's the end of the first period and Sinden tells Fergie to give the pep talk. He says, 'Someone in this room has got to get that sonovabitch Kharlamov.' Clarke tells me, 'I'm looking around the room and I came to the conclusion he was talking to me.' At one stage in the second period, Clarke is in forechecking and he lays a wicked two-hander, on his ankle. Goodbye Kharlamov.

"Afterwards, Clarke looked like an angelic choirboy. I said to him, that was a wicked two-hander, and he just looks up at me and says, 'Mr. Beddoes, if I hadn't learned to lay on what you call a wicked two-hander, I would never have left Flin Flon, Manitoba."

"Having Kharlamov out of the lineup made it a little easier for us," said Clarke. "It's not something I would've done in an NHL game, at least I hope I wouldn't. But that situation, against Soviet players, at that stage in the series, with everything that was happening, it was necessary."

The Canadians again opened strongly in what was one of the best-played games of the series. They opened the scoring just 4:09 into the game, when winger Ron Ellis and Park won the battle along the boards and Ellis centred to Phil Esposito in the slot. He easily beat goalie Vladislav Tretiak.

Park was victimized on the tying goal, which arrived just six minutes later, when he stumbled at the Canadian blue line, allowing winger Alexandr Yakushev a breakaway. He tucked a shot between the pads of Tony Esposito. Park was snakebitten again when the Soviets went ahead, 2-1, at 16:27. A pass caromed off Park's skate and ultimately wound up on the stick of centre Vladimir Petrov. It was a power-play goal, with Bill White in the penalty box.

"He had a few problems on the first couple of goals," said

Sinden, "but in the last two games Park really started to play well. In Canada, he hadn't played that well. His wife had had a baby when we were in Toronto, and next to Bobby Orr he was the outstanding defenceman of the time. But he came on.

"Bill White and Pat Stapleton were steady, and Serge, who played with a cracked bone in his ankle, and Lapointe also played really well. We also got a tremendous series out of Gary Bergman, who played with Park. Bergman was a guy we picked, but we weren't sure he could make it."

Esposito scored his second goal of the game to tie it 2-2, squeezing a shot through a scramble, at 17:34 of the opening period, after Savard and Parise had acquired the puck at the blue line.

After the Soviets had almost doubled the shots on the Canadians in the second period, holding a wide 13-7 edge, the tie was finally broken early in the third period, at 2:13. Gilbert intercepted a pass behind the net, emerged from the corner and lifted a backhand shot between the pads of Tretiak. The lead survived just three minutes, though, until Yakushev scored his second goal on a power play, with a setup from Alexandr Maltsev.

It was then that Tony Esposito, who had complained of feeling ill, really began to shine, making at least six brilliant saves to maintain the tie. The Soviets had begun to really press, but midway through the period, the game was halted to change ends. Whatever momentum they built was siphoned out, and order was restored, the teams playing tight, thrilling hockey, waiting for a break.

"I didn't feel that well before the game," said Tony Esposito. "But it was such a long road trip, I think I was just rundown. But we all had to suck it up. It took a lot out of guys to come back the way we did."

A near riot almost occurred at 16:26, though, when Bergman and Soviet centre Boris Mikhailov came together behind the Canadians' goal. What followed was a fight that emptied both benches. Bergman had rammed Mikhailov into the boards and the two began shoving, their arms wrapped around each other. While they jostled, the Soviet began kicking Bergman in the shins, while Bergman banged Mikhailov's head against the wire mesh atop the boards. That prompted the exodus from the benches, but miraculously a major brawl did not erupt.

"Bergman was mad as hell," recalled White. "This guy had kicked him and Bergman was going to kill him."

Once peace was restored, less than two minutes later, the game now into its final three minutes, the stage was set for more of Henderson's heroics. He didn't disappoint.

From a faceoff in the Canadian zone, Clarke won the draw back to Lapointe, who slid a pass behind the net to Savard, who then hit a streaking Henderson in flight at centre ice. From there, rushing rapidly in on two defencemen, Henderson attempted to deke by both, was hit, pushed the puck around defenceman Gynady Tsygankov, eased by him, and then, while falling to the ice, squeezed a shot between the arm and body of Tretiak for the winning goal, at 17:54. It was Henderson's sixth goal of the series.

Final score: Team Canada 4, Soviet Union 3.

"What a goal," said Eagleson. "The score was tied and Henderson came down on a one-on-two. Then all of a sudden he's in the clear. It was incredible. I couldn't believe it. It was a nothing play that turned into a winning goal."

It's a goal, too, that Henderson remembers as being perhaps being the best he scored in his career — and very nearly as dramatic as the one that would follow in game eight.

"I had never beaten anyone one-on-two in my life and never did again," said Henderson. "Can you believe it? A one on two. I beat two defencemen, then Tretiak. I had never done that even in practice. It was by far the best goal I scored. Ever. If we don't win that game, the eighth game doesn't mean a hill of beans, either."

The line of Clarke, Ellis and Henderson was the only unit to survive the series intact, together through all eight games, and it was the most consistent line. They combined the assets of offensive skill and sound checking ability with determination and speed. They could skate, handle the puck, and they played well in their own zone. Oddly enough, they were the last three players selected, Clarke the very last, for the team.

"I think that line was the key to the series," said Ferguson. "At first we didn't even know if it was going to be a line, but then Clarke really came on. We put them together, and they stuck."

"Henderson had looked good from the very beginning," said Sinden. "This was the type of hockey he seemed to be best suited for, too. He was an excellent checking, scoring forward, who wasn't aggressive in the NHL, but became quite aggressive during that series. We had invited thirty-five players and we had to make sure we covered all the bases, that we had the top scorers, and some players are better suited for these things."

"I'd say Henderson played pretty decent," said Park, "but I wouldn't say he was the best on the team. His line was pretty strong. He had Clarke and Ellis, and I'd say Clarke was playing the strongest at that time."

"Our line played very well," said Ellis. "I think we were fortunate, we were probably in the last five of the thirty-five players to be named to the team, but we played hard, worked hard and our styles were helpful to us. All three of us played a good, two-way game against the Russians. That's the type of people you need, and I think that's a reason we were successful."

"Right from the start they put us together," said Clarke. "We were three guys who never missed a practice. We all felt if we were given a chance to play we could play well. But we knew we had to work. We never had a bad practice. We had to produce so the coaches would notice us. We probably had an advantage in terms of conditioning over the Espositos and Mahovliches. We didn't have reputations and had to work harder.

"They told me afterwards that I was picked because Walter Tkaczuk refused to go. But I think Eagleson had a lot of influence on my being chosen, too. He knew me and he knew I'd work hard, be competitive. They were looking for guys like that."

"The series was very good for Clarke, Ellis and myself," said Henderson. "We functioned well as a unit, and over the series I think we developed into the best line. Espo was our best player and our inspirational leader, no question, but I think we were the best line. Anyone we played against in the series we dominated. Our line surprised a lot of people and, of course, we scored the big goals.

"I don't think we were in the first twenty players selected for the team, that's for sure, but I would've been really disappointed if we hadn't been part of the thirty-five selected."

As Hull recalled, too, it almost seemed as if Henderson had a special invitation to participate.

"It's like he says," said Hull. "He was destined to score those winning goals."

And the final destiny would be met two nights later, September 28, 1972...

CHAPTER TEN

One for Dad
and Country

"After we won the seventh game, we all went out to the ballet the next night," recalled organizer Alan Eagleson. "The guys didn't like it very much, but it was something to do, just to pass the time. Well, in the middle of the show, there's an intermission and that's when we heard about the officials. I couldn't believe it. I just said right then, 'Either we get the right refs for the final game, or we're going home.'

"I remember, it's half time in the play and Arthur Lang, who was sent by (Prime Minister) Trudeau, says there's no way we'll be going home. We walked across the hall and I told him that if we don't get a fair shake and have to play with the two Eastern Bloc referees, we're not going to play.

"I said to him, 'If you can convince the players to stay, then go ahead.' But most of the players were standing there at the time and they were just as upset as I was."

The eighth game in this historic summit would be remembered for many things — the winning goal, the dramatics, the comeback, the sheer brilliance of the spectacle — but it would also be remembered for several other incidents, some seamy, some just plain peculiar. In the space of forty-eight hours, between games, the true essence of international hockey would be neatly captured, from the political meddlings to the outstanding performances. It's just difficult to tell sometimes which gains a greater prominence.

But after the Canadians had battled back, winning the seventh game to deadlock the series at 3-3-1, the unsavoury side of the international game and the Soviets' involvement in it began to surface, beginning that night at the Bolshoi Ballet with the news of a suspicious change of officials for the eighth and final game.

After the debacle that was game six, when the Canadians won 3-2 but were incredibly angered over the work of West German officials Josef Kompalla and Franz Baader — who gave them thiry-one minutes in penalties and the Soviets just four — they were promised those two would not officiate again in the series. Remember the Canadians had also endured their incompetence in an exhibition game in Sweden.

But there was a change of plans — Soviet style. All of a sudden, the Soviets were insisting that the agreement pertaining to the use of officials was good only for the seventh game and there was no guarantee for game eight. Their preference was clear, too. Team Canada, meanwhile, had figured that Sweden's Uve Dahlberg and Czechoslovakia's Rudy Bata, a far more acceptable pairing, would officiate the final game, as they had in game seven.

And now there was a very real threat of the Canadians returning home, the series never to be completed. It was a bargaining ploy, mostly posturing obviously. The Canadians had reached the precipice of their comeback, were seemingly on the verge of victory, and desperately wanted to prove their supremacy and polish their pride. Still, there existed a sincere desire to hastily retreat home rather than give in to the angling of the Soviets. Of course, the threat hit the Soviets directly where they lived. If the Canadians left, the Soviets would not receive the $200,000 in European television money earmarked for them.

"We had our choice of referees in game eight," said Eagleson, "so we selected Dahlberg and Bata. But (Andrei) Starovoitov (Eagleson's Soviet counterpart) told me we couldn't have Dahlberg because he was sick. But I had just talked to him about an hour earlier and he was fine. So I went and saw him and I said, 'What's going on here?' And he told me Starovoitov had told him if he refereed the game it would be the last game he would work."

An agreement was finally struck, just after 1 p.m. on the afternoon of the final game, September 28, 1972. Each team would select one official, with Team Canada allowed Bata, the Soviets' getting Kompalla, their choice. All of a sudden, too, a new emotion had entered into proceedings. Hatred. Before, the stakes were high and the competition predictably intense, but now the Canadians were an even angrier, more hostile team, intent on vindication. More than a week in the Soviet Union, subjected to its peculiarities and the mysterious hijinks, had left them bitter and determined.

"It was a bunch of political bullshit," said winger Wayne Cashman.

Nevertheless, they were subject to the laws of the land, playing under International Ice Hockey Federation rules in the Soviet Union. You take your chances, hope for the best, but don't ever expect a problem-free working arrangement. Murphy's Law could have been born in Russia.

"It didn't matter what happened, though, because the confidence level of the team was way up and we knew we would win on the ice," said backup goalie Eddie Johnston. "We believed we always had enough to win. But the pressure in that game was so incredible. Guys were so intense, so pumped up."

Twenty-seven days after the first chapter in hockey history had been written, the conclusion was to be authored, with a surprise ending very few had foreseen. And it would be dripping with drama, compelling entertainment, which virtually brought a country to a standstill, waiting in breathless anticipation. The series that had begun with the foolishly high expectations in Canada of a romp, a humiliating sweep, well, those sentiments had long since vanished and given way to a new wave of emotions — uncertainty and anxiety and an excitement. The Soviets had proven themselves very worthy opponents, and time had allowed Team Canada to develop into the same. They were about as close as two teams could get, and now there were sixty minutes to settle the issue, to sort out bragging rights, to salvage pride and prestige. It was our best against their best for the first time, and winning was everything.

This was, after all, a series Canadians had long awaited, suffered annually watching gritty, amateur Canadian teams dismantled by the Soviets in the Olympics and the world championships. Worse still, because Canada had not won an Olympic gold medal in hockey since 1952, or the world title since 1961, the Soviets considered themselves the best. Sure it was propaganda, but there hadn't previously been a forum to settle the argument, either. This was that chance to clarify hockey supremacy once and for all.

"What pressure there was that game," said winger Yvon Cournoyer. "There was pressure on us because we were always supposed to win this series, but there was pressure on them, too. They were at home and being close wasn't going to be good enough for them, or us. They certainly didn't want to lose, not after taking such a big lead. And there was so much stuff — political stuff — happening all the time.

"But, as with any series, the games are won on the ice, and we knew we could win it. We knew our backs were still to the wall. We just had to win."

There are also a couple of old allies in sports — momentum and confidence — and Team Canada owned a sizable share of both. They had twice won, in games six and seven, when a loss would have decided the outcome of the series and firmly believed they could defy the odds of winning three of four games on Moscow ice to complete the comeback. They had the momentum of two impressive wins, the confidence of seeing marked improvement in their play, and they had the added motivation of being angered and frustrated.

"I think that maybe our team became overconfident after the fifth game," explained Soviet centre Boris Mikhailov. "Going into the eighth game, we knew we had to win. There was much pressure to succeed on both teams."

"We had Phil Esposito as our spiritual leader," said Dennis

Hull, "And we had a guy like Bobby Clarke, who was quietly confident. I think the main thought was we'll show those Canadians who were against us. That was a really hurtful feeling. But before that final game, we realized how the support back home had snowballed. And then before the eighth game we got this unbelievable telegram. Those fans in Moscow, they were part of our group. I couldn't believe how supportive they were. They made more noise than all the Russians put together."

Team Canada coach Harry Sinden made only two lineup changes for the final game, maintaining his goaltending rotation and starting Ken Dryden, who had won in game six. But Sinden promised he would make a quick switch to Tony Esposito if necessary. He also dressed left winger Frank Mahovlich, whose skating skills were better suited to the larger ice surface. He replaced Bill Goldsworthy.

"After we had settled on the refs," said Eagleson, "I figured Tony would get the start in goal, but no, it was Kenny Dryden. Those coaches certainly knew what they were doing."

"I was a little surprised," admitted Tony Esposito. "The seventh game was my best of the series. I felt my game was really coming together. I was at the top of my game, but they made the switch anyway. Dryden always had a tough time playing against the Europeans. He's more of an angle goalie and there's a lot of lateral movement to their game. He had a lot of problems, but I was ready. I knew they'd make a change if we got in trouble."

"My only memory of between games," said Dryden, "was between the seventh and eighth games. It was the most difficult day I've ever spent. I have never felt that way between games.

The nerves. We had all played championship games before and you like to equate the situations, but my legs and my stomach reacted differently. I couldn't escape that jellied feeling. It might leave for half an hour or so, but it would always come back. I never felt that way again."

The Soviets' hopes were incredibly buoyed by the return of star winger Valeri Kharlamov, who had missed the seventh game because of that ankle injury. To make room for Kharlamov, perhaps their most dangerous forward, the Soviets' deleted veteran defenceman Alexandr Ragulin, whose lack of speed had been exploited the past couple of games.

"No one had to say too much before that game," said Hull. "Everyone was ready. Everyone knew what they had to do."

The final game would be outstanding, but it would still be remembered for its other components, for events that occurred on and off the ice. The good, the bad, the unbelievable.

* * *

Whatever apprehensions — no, fears — Team Canada had over the calibre of officiating were realized early in the opening period when minor penalties were assessed in succession to defenceman Bill White and centre Peter Mahovlich, leaving them two men short for one minute and twenty-four seconds. A deep hole. The penalties weren't absolutely bad calls, but they were questionable, and it was early.

Anyway, with the penalty box loading up, the Soviets opened the scoring at 3:34, with big winger Alexandr Yakushev parked in front of the goal, snapping a rebound past Dryden. Less than a minute later, all hell broke loose.

Truculent winger J.P. Parise was given an interference penalty for bumping Alexandr Maltsev at 4:10. Parise was so incensed with the decision that he first muttered obscenities, then slammed his stick on the ice, breaking the lumber. Kompalla immediately added a ten-minute misconduct for this indiscretion.

Further enraged, Parise built up a short head of steam and charged crazily toward Kompalla, who was standing by the penalty box. As he approached and swung by, Parise feigned whacking Kompalla over the head with his stick, his actions earning him a game misconduct, which prompted a cascade of debris from the Canadian bench, including a stool, a chair and several towels.

"That game, the refereeing was the most dreadful I've ever experienced," recalled Parise. "During the game, the frustration just built up to such a high level. That incident, I did it for a couple of reasons. One, I wanted to let them know that we had had enough. If they're not going to play fair, we won't. It was war. It was bullshit that Kompalla was the referee in the first place and not Dahlberg. It was just more of their bullshit.

"The first call just before that was questionable. Then we get the second penalty while we're still killing a penalty. Then he calls me. It was a good check. So I say, 'What the fuck! Are you kidding me?' Then he gives me ten minutes, and now I'm saying, 'You son of a bitch!'

"I was going to hit him right over the head, but between starting and reaching where he was standing, I thought about what would happen, and I would probably have been banned for life. I had enough sense to pull back.

"When I got kicked out of the game, I felt like such a shit. You know, you're part of a team and you have a certain responsibility to the team. But no one said anything to me. I think they were happy I had done it."

If nothing else, it reaffirmed the Canadians' resolve, and it tested both their poise and discipline. They didn't waver. A few minutes later, too, Soviet defenceman Evgeny (Gynady) Tsygankov was sent to the penalty box and Team Canada pulled even on the ensuing power play, Phil Esposito slamming in the rebound of a Brad Park point shot at 6:45.

Predictably, on a night when the officiating was being closely scrutinized and criticized, both team's power-play units were effective, which simply added to the controversy and the open hostility.

Midway through the opening period, at 13:10, defenceman Vladimir Lutchenko restored the Soviets' lead, driving a screen shot from the point past a helpless Dryden on, you guessed it, another power play. The determination with which the Canadians were playing, though, was just beginning to show, and before the period was over they had drawn even again, Park completing a nice passing play with Hull and Jean Ratelle at 16:59.

"We were playing pretty well," said Cournoyer. "The big thing is we got through the first few minutes of the game, with all the penalties and stuff, but we still managed to keep our composure."

"You know in a game like that," said Sinden, "anything can happen. But we were certain we could beat them and we were intent on making it awfully tough on them. We played a pretty good period."

Now, after twenty-seven days, seven games and one period, the series was still even. Just forty minutes remained...

"There was a lot of tension," said Cournoyer, "but when you're confident like we were, it takes care of that. And we had all been through similar situations."

Just twenty-one seconds into the second period, though, the Soviets stunned the Canadians with an early, somewhat bizarre goal. Unlike the North American rinks, the Luzhniki arena was not equipped with Plexiglas around the boards and behind the goal. Instead, behind the nets were huge sheets of springy wire mesh, which often gave goalies fits. Add Dryden to the list.

On the goal, Yakushev drifted a shot high off the mesh and it sprung back out crazily toward the blue line, where Vladimir Shadrin drove it behind a startled Dryden. Sensing they could put the Canadians away, the Soviets pressed hard to expand their lead, but Dryden was excellent. Undaunted, the Canadians continued to battle back, erasing the Soviets' third lead at 10:32. White snuck down the right side from the point to tap in a clever pass from Rod Gilbert, who had drawn all the attention to the other side of the net.

The Soviets were persistent, though, and their intense pressure finally resulted in goals before the period was over. At 11:43, less than two minutes after White had tied the score, a lost faceoff in the Team Canada zone led to a goal by Yakushev. Another penalty, this one to Pat Stapleton, led to the Soviets' fifth goal, and third of the night on the power play. Just fourteen seconds before Stapleton was to return to the ice, Vasiliev banked a shot in off a leg at 16:44.

End of two periods: Soviet Union 5, Team Canada 3.

"We had fallen way behind," said Sinden, "but we had still played quite well, I thought. We were getting lots of shots, but Tretiak was playing great.

"I remember we talked between the second and third periods and I told them, 'We're down 5-3, but we don't need two goals in five minutes. Let's try and get one goal and if we can get through the first ten minutes in at least no worse a position, we'll be in good shape.' That was the most important thing we could do.

"If we're two down with ten minutes to go, we could gamble a bit. But to gamble early and get down by three, it would be lights out."

In the dressing room, there was no panic. The players remained calm, though there was high anxiety in the air and constant interruptions.

"In the dressing room, all of us were saying, 'Don't worry, we've got it now, we're going to win,'" said Phil Esposito. "There wasn't a negative thought."

"That was the only time I ever went into the dressing room between periods," said Eagleson. "I remember going in, the cops had just pushed around Ambassador Ford's wife amd my wife, Nancy, after they had reached around to pat Henderson on the back and wish the players good luck.

"I was livid. I had just seen these guys pushing a couple of women around. I had seen Alexandr Gresko (Soviet's international hockey representative) earlier and I said to him, 'Wouldn't it be nice if we come back and it ended in a tie?' But he says to me if there was a tie we would lose on goal differential. Going into that game, they had scored twenty-seven goals and we had scored twenty-six.

"I went into the dressing room going nuts, screaming. I was yelling, 'If we get a goal early, they'll fall apart!' I went absolutely berserk for about twenty seconds."

Eagleson's impassioned plea for a comeback has not faded from the players' memory, either. Interestingly, they recall the events before the final period with almost as much fondness and accuracy as the events that would follow. Almost.

"I remember Alan Eagleson coming into the dressing room after the second period," said Hull. "He said to us, 'You guys win this thing and you all get a new car.' You know, I think he said it in the heat of what was going on, but I remember that. No one else seems to remember that, including Eagleson, but for some reason I remember that.

"I remember the enormity of what was going to happen in the next twenty minutes. Before the third period, the Russians had put extra water on the ice when they flooded it. So, Harry said we were going to wait until it was frozen. And Eagleson came in to find out what was going on. The refs were blowing their whistles, but Harry still made us wait until it was frozen."

"I have vivid memories of that game," said winger Ron Ellis. "We were down 5-3 and we could've been frustrated and upset, but the one thing I will always remember about that game is the real confidence that existed. Everyone just believed we were going to go out and do it. I remember between periods, we could've said, 'Well, we came this far and blew it,' but there was a real quiet confidence there. No one was saying too much, except that we knew what we had to do. I'll always remember that time between the periods. It's very special to me."

"After the second period, trailing 5-3," recalled Dryden, "there wasn't a negative feeling in the dressing room. There was the sense that we've played seven games and two periods, we have one period left, let's just see, that this is the final go-round, let's just go out and play."

"Losing just never fit into the equation, it's that simple," said winger Paul Henderson. "We were down 5-3, not too excited, but we felt if we got one goal early, and we didn't given them one, we would be right back in it and we would win. The thought of losing just had never crossed anyone's mind.

"It's because everything was there by then, the confidence in the players, the coaches, the conditioning, and we had come together as a team."

Viewing proceedings from a much different perspective was Parise, who had been banished from the game in the opening minutes for his behaviour. Allowed to dress only seventeen players, without Parise they now had just three lines and one extra forward.

"When we went into that final period my confidence was down a bit," said Parise. "When you're out on the ice, you feel you can make a contribution, but when you're sitting out, you feel a little helpless. But I actually started to relax once the period started. I mean, on that team, anyone who takes your place is going to be pretty good. I had a good feeling."

The Canadians took Sinden's advice to heart, too, and played a controlled, disciplined early third period and were rewarded with grand results. It was then, too, that the leaders reemerged. Bobby Clarke continued his diligent, hardnosed play with linemates Ellis and Henderson. And big Phil Esposito simply refused to allow the team to lose.

"It was Phil's finest hour," said Sinden. "And he didn't complain too bad in the series, either. But it was like Phil just wasn't going to let us lose that series. He did the right things at the right moments. He wasn't about to let us go."

Esposito was more than just an emotional, spiritual leader, too, although his speech in Vancouver had obviously been a turning point for Team Canada, a sort of rallying cry. But he also led by example on the ice, wearing his heart on his sleeve for all to see, his heart as big as the Maple Leaf on his chest. It was more than just a hockey series to him. There was pride involved.

Earlier in the game, Esposito, who was widely regarded for his offensive skills and perhaps not as respected as a player of his calibre should have been, showed the sort of determination with which he was playing when he slid through the crease, behind a fallen Dryden, to block a shot and save a goal. It was significant then, but few realized how big a save it would become. A three-goal deficit would have killed their hopes.

"The ironic part," said journalist Dick Beddoes, "is Phil turns out to be the leader, and we'd called him a money grubber at the start of the series."

"The Canadian team had many smart players," said Mikhailov. "Because Henderson scored many goals — many were game winners — he was very valuable, but he was not the best player on the team. The Esposito brothers, Park, Savard, Lapointe were all better players. Phil Esposito was a great player."

More to the point, as Sinden had said earlier, when they named their thirty-five-man roster in early August, they had tried to foresee every necessity. Esposito gave them heart, and

Henderson gave them the solid two-way player who ultimately turned out to be a hero. Call it destiny.

Anyway, Esposito provided the pivotal goal Team Canada required to mount its comeback, scoring just 2:27 into the final period to narrow the deficit to 5-4. Peter Mahovlich had worked hard to acquire the puck in the corner, passed in front, and Esposito knocked the puck to the ice and deposited a second shot behind Tretiak.

"The goal I scored early, I was in the slot, the pass came up high, I grabbed it, bounced it once, and put it in the net," explained Esposito.

A minute later, the first real fight of the series broke out, when Rod Gilbert and Evgeny Mishakov dropped their gloves and briefly fought. If Esposito's goal had shown there was fight left in Team Canada, then Gilbert's fight drove the point home as subtly as, well, a punch in the mouth.

Thusly inspired by the two events, the Canadians continued to play well in their own end, but were creating offensive chances, too. Esposito also had a big hand in the tying goal, which arrived at 12:56 and created a bigger stir than anyone could imagine. Fending off two Soviet defenders, Esposito still managed a tough shot on Tretiak, with the rebound going to Cournoyer, who tapped it in.

"We had managed to score early, then tie it up after ten minutes," said Sinden. "It was all a bonus as far as we had been thinking. We hadn't gone out trying to tie it up early. The thinking was, we just wanted to be in a position to win it in the last ten minutes."

"There's one thing I remember," said Hull. "It was in the third period, and I had looked up into the box above the ice that held the president of the USSR. I don't think the fans could see him, but all these Politburo members were clapping their hands, thinking they had won the series and beaten the dastardly Canadians. Then all of a sudden we've got it tied up."

Another major ruckus ensued, immediately after Cournoyer's shot had crossed the goal line. While obviously a goal, the red goal light didn't blink on. Manning the switch that night was a fellow not beyond suspicion named Viktor Dombrowski, a Soviet referee who in the years to follow would earn the same regard from Canadian hockey teams as Kompalla before him. He has long been a nemesis of Canadian teams internationally, and that night was for a time public enemy number one, though he insisted afterwards the light switch simply didn't work.

"I remember we had just changed ends," said Eagleson, "and finally Cournoyer scored to tie it, but that's when the goal light didn't come on. I saw the referee point to the goal, but I thought I had better get to the announcer — who was a guy from Edmonton, the first Canadian to ever defect to Russia — and get him to quickly announce the goal.

"I jumped over two rows of seats to get down there. I was going full tilt and probably looked like a madman when this soldier grabs me. They didn't know who I was, or what I was doing. They just grabbed me."

As Eagleson leapt over the seats, he was confronted by several soldiers. He was soon involved in a shoving match and was losing it. Before long, there were at least half a dozen soldiers surrounding Eagleson, ready to take him away.

"Peter Mahovlich was on the ice at the time," continued

Eagleson. "He was the only one tall enough to see over the boards and into the mote they have around the rink and see what was going on. Well, Peter saw it and just hurdled over the boards and hit one guy over the shoulder with his stick."

"Some people are still mad at me — all those who don't like Alan," deadpanned Mahovlich. "But it was a funny situation. You don't even think about what you're doing, you just react. I just climbed over the boards and all of a sudden here I am standing on a cement floor, sliding around with all these soldiers standing there. I never hit them, though. I just threatened them. They didn't know what to make of all this. I mean, no one stands up to them, especially at a sporting event."

"Well, they finally got me out of there," continued Eagleson, "and as I was walking across the ice, I just told the world we were number one — but I used the wrong finger."

The incident greatly angered the Soviets and several Canadian diplomats, and even bothered some of the Canadian-media delegation, which was not polite in its reviews, with columnist John Robertson, then of the *Montreal Star*, referring to Eagleson as a "diplomatic disaster." The single-finger salute did not earn Eagleson many supporters, though the incident was soon vastly overshadowed. And it was just another byproduct of the first-ever summit, further evidence of how it had gripped people and twisted their emotions. Rationality wasn't preserved. It was a series, after all, that had an almost alluring mix of the unexpected, the bizarre and the wonderful.

"We behaved over there like Grey Cup fans used to behave," said Beddoes. "It was the grand national drunk, overseas version. What Eagle and the players did was anarchy in the Soviet Union.

We were 2,700 surrounded by 270 million. But when you're over there, embattled, a part of it all, you don't feel like you're acting so boorish. But clearly we were misbehaving. You just don't feel it at the time."

All this, too, because the goal light didn't switch on. It might seem trivial, in hindsight, an overreaction, but in the spirit of the moment, winning was everything and Team Canada had finally mounted the summit it had begun to climb twenty-seven days earlier. The goal light was functioning, too, and before the night was over Team Canada would provide comrade Dombrowski with another chance to test it.

"At that point," added Eagleson, "I was happy with a tie."

The Soviets were visibly unsettled by the incidents of the third period — the two goals, the fight, the off-ice scuffle — and appeared to be in something of a state of shock when play resumed. Team Canada, though, was bubbling with emotion. They were charged up. Electric. It almost seemed, too, that the reeling Soviets were now content with a tie, especially since they could claim victory afterwards on the goal differential.

"I remember," said Parise, "with about two minutes left in the game, and we're tied 5-5, the Russian head of sports says to Eagleson, 'If it finishes in a tie, we win because we have more goals in the series.' And Eagleson just says to him, 'Fuck off. You haven't won anything yet.' We all felt that way. 'You haven't won anything yet.'"

Esposito and Henderson weren't done, neither the comeback nor the dramatics complete. And with less than one minute remaining in the game, thirty-four seconds to be precise, perhaps the most memorable moment in Canadian sporting history, perhaps even in just plain Canadian history, occurred.

"Henderson has scored for Canada..."

"On the play," recalled Sinden, "I couldn't get Phil off the ice, which wasn't unusual for him. I knew Phil so well from Boston. He was always out there when he shouldn't have been and we had just started a line change. Their top line was coming on and we had been playing Clarke, Ellis and Henderson against them. But the puck was in their end, and with the wide rink, well, Phil just didn't come off — thank goodness."

"I was tired," said Cournoyer, who was on the line with Esposito and Peter Mahovlich at the time. "I was going to go to the bench, but for some reason I just changed my mind. I don't know why really, but if I hadn't we probably wouldn't have scored. I was going to go to the bench, but I turned and went back to the boards. I guess the reason was because the bench was so far away, on the other side, and the rinks are wide. I was on the other side of the rink."

"I had never done it before in my life and I have never done it since," began Henderson, "but I called Peter off the ice. It was hard to believe. Why did Peter ever come off the ice? But I had this feeling I could score the winning goal. Unbelievable."

"It was one of those situations that just happens and you're glad you did it," said Peter Mahovlich. "I had been on for a while and I didn't want to go in to the offensive zone if I couldn't make it back to check. Paul was up and ready on the bench, he called me, and I gave him the nod to go."

"The (Soviet) defenceman got the puck behind his net and threw it around the boards, just hoping to clear it out of his zone," continued Cournoyer. "But because I had decided to stay on the ice, I was standing there. On the boards. Maybe he hadn't seen me come back, I don't know. But I intercepted the pass and I saw Paul coming from the bench, down the left side, and Phil was with him. But I missed Paul with the pass..."

"I sure did call to Yvon for the puck," continued Henderson, "but it was behind me, and when I reached back I got tripped up and crashed into the boards. I got back up and Phil just whacked at the puck..."

"I was on the ice a long time," said Esposito. "The puck came out from the corner — it was loose. I was in the faceoff circle and I snapped it and Tretiak made the save, but Henderson was right there for the rebound..."

"I had moved out in front of the goal," said Henderson. "Tretiak kicked the rebound out and I just tried to slide it along the ice, but darned if he didn't get a piece of that one, too. But the rebound came right back to me, and I had half the net to shoot at. I just flipped it over him."

"Henderson has scored for Canada..."

With just thirty-four seconds remaining in the eighth and final game, Henderson had given Team Canada a 6-5 lead they would not relinquish. And as he raised his arms high in the air, he was embraced in person by Cournoyer and in spirit by a nation. It was the biggest goal a Canadian player had ever scored, and it perhaps remains so.

"The first reaction, the first emotion," said Henderson, "was total elation. But in 1968, my father died, and he wanted me to be a hockey player so bad. He influenced my life so much that when I scored, in all that elation, there was a touch of melancholy for a second, and then it was over. I just thought,

'I wish Dad were here to see me score that goal.'"

"Watching that goal go in," said Esposito, "it was like slow motion in my mind at the time it happened. There was a lot of elation, that's for sure. We had won the series."

"I was right behind Paul when he scored," said Cournoyer. "I was glad I had changed my mind. If the ice hadn't been so large, maybe I would've gone to the bench. With me staying on and Paul coming off the bench…who knows what makes it happen? Maybe it's something that just has to happen. We could try that a hundred times and it would never work, but this time it did."

"I just wish I had seen the look on the faces of those Politburo members in the box when Henderson scored," added Hull. "I didn't think to look up there, but I'm sure their expressions had changed. When Henderson scored, it was like a big piano had been lifted off our backs. Everyone felt elated. Even before he scored, and time ticked away, I felt we would be remembered just for the way we came back. And then when we scored…it was amazing."

There were still thirty-four seconds remaining, of course, which in this series was sufficient time for a comeback. But having erased four deficits, the Canadians were not about to allow their lead to disappear.

"I have no on-ice recollection," said Dryden, "except of sprinting down the ice when the shot went in. But I don't remember anticipating the play, I just remember jumping out of the starting blocks and hurrying down the ice. I remember the celebration, then thinking, my God, there are still thirty-four seconds to go, I've got to get a hold of myself."

"It's funny," continued Peter Mahovlich. "Paul goes out on the ice and bang, he scores the winner. But as it turns out, I was back out for the final thirty-four seconds. At that juncture in the series I hadn't played that much on a regular basis, except to kill penalties. But I was getting a lot of work in that last game. I got to play a lot of left wing on a line with Phil and Cournoyer. It's funny how things happen. But I didn't even see that goal. Like I said, I was tired and that's why I came off. But I sure responded to the cheering of our fans."

The Canadians did manage to efficiently survive the final seconds and win the summit series, 4-3-1, though not quite the way most had envisioned when it began. But then, the unexpected turn for the dramatic was one of the many charms. Victory, however close, was gratifying for Team Canada.

"Those final thirty-four seconds were the longest in my life," said Eagleson. "And the Russians had a good chance right at the end and almost tied it. But what a game. What a series."

When the buzzer finally sounded, Team Canada again spilled over the boards. For a long while they embraced one another, as the 2,700 Canadian fans cheered wildly and a nation half a world away did much the same, singing *O Canada* as one. The vast majority at Luzhniki arena understandably were not happy as they quietly departed.

"Losing that game was the worst moment of my career," said Mikhailov. "I had a sick feeling for a long time."

"The series was never hatred," said Dennis Hull. "I mean, when you saw how talented they were, you had to admire the skills they had. But I think the Soviets were very disappointed when they lost. They hadn't waited all those years to lose. I think they were expecting to win."

Meanwhile, in the Canadian dressing room, a celebration that would carry on long into the night and early morning, at home and abroad, had only just begun, as emotions scampered from elation, to relief, to more utter joy. The odyssey that had begun twenty-seven days earlier was at last complete, and victory was sweet.

"I've never seen grown men cry like that when it was over," said Johnston. "The series was so draining, and it was such a relief when it was finally over. To come back so far, to win, to make it so dramatic, the emotions alternated from excitement to relief. And maybe everyone was just a wee bit exhausted — mentally, especially — at that time."

"Actually, it was impossible to really enjoy the moment afterwards," said Parise. "I would have liked to have closed the dressing-room door for about fifteen minutes or so and just sat back and enjoyed it. Let it sink in. But all these people came in and it was kind of impossible to savour it. I would have liked to have just sat there with my teammates and looked around at each other and realize what we did. But there really wasn't the opportunity to do that. There was just too much going on."

"I didn't have much time to enjoy it," said Park. "I didn't get back to the dressing room in time, really. I had been brought up to the television booth as one of the game stars, and the interview was being transmitted back to Canada. I don't remember a thing I said on television, either.

"But when I got back to the dressing room everyone was already pretty pumped. We had redeemed our honour. But we weren't breaking up right after that, either. We were going from there to Prague the next morning to play an exhibition game."

Before departing for Czechoslovakia, though, there was still more partying to be done, a special banquet held that night at the Metropole Hotel to honour both teams. But only one stayed for the duration. Actually, recollections of the party were understandably quite foggy seventeen years later — and no doubt the morning after.

"At the Intourist Hotel, the bar was jammed," said journalist Dick Beddoes. "It was New Year's Eve, Times Square, New York. In the dressing room, though, Anisin came in with this ill-wrapped parcel. He elbowed his way through the crowd to Phil and gave the parcel to him. It was a *samovar* (kettle) used to boil water. But the Soviets knew who the best player was and they showed their manners. Phil says, 'Gee, I don't have anything to give him.' He's naked and runs out of the room and grabs a stick for the guy. 'My mother in the Sault taught me some manners,' he said. It was in the dressing room, too, that Paul delivered his famous quote: 'Until I scored that goal, I didn't know the difference between democracy and communism.' The partying that night, though, was incredible."

"At the celebration," said Gilbert, "the whole Soviet team was there for the first part, but then they removed them all. I guess they didn't want us to get to them."

"I remember we partied a lot," recalled White. "We were leaving the next day (at 4:30 a.m.) and I had asked Stapleton to wake me up. I was rooming with my wife, but I had asked Pat to make sure I got up. Well, he didn't. So I wake up the next morning and I realize I'm late. So I run out into the hallway and I see Eagleson's father. He looks at me and I say, 'Where is everybody?' And he says, 'They've all gone to the airport.' They had left without me. I guess they figured everyone would get up."

"They had it all set up that the two teams would get together after the game," said Hull, "but only two Russians came. I think it was Yakushev and Tretiak. The rest of the guys stayed away. We celebrated all night. The next day at the airport, before we left for Czechoslovakia to play that final exhibition game, Harry lined us up and he would go down the line looking at us and saying, 'You can play, you can't play.' We all were feeling pretty awful. Yeah, I got to play in that game (a 3-3 tie). I think the Czechs were as happy as we were. They were amazed that we had won."

"To see that puck go in with thirty-four seconds remaining, it was an all-time high for everyone on that team and no one will ever forget it," said Johnston. "Even today the players and fans remember that series, where they were when Paul scored that goal. It was more than just a hockey series. Basically it was war."

"Henderson has scored for Canada..."

CHAPTER ELEVEN

Seventeen Years Later

"**W**hen we won game eight, it was like a big elephant had been lifted off our backs," offered Team Canada winger Rod Gilbert. "If we had lost, I was staying in Russia. I would have gone to Siberia or something."

The flight carrying Team Canada arrived at Dorval Airport in Montreal in the early evening of October 1, 1972. A crowd estimated at 10,000, which included Prime Minister Pierre Elliott Trudeau, was waiting on the tarmac, waving flags and carrying banners. They were on hand to greet the team of destiny, the team of heroes. Oh, how the passing of time had altered that perspective.

A few weeks earlier, Team Canada had been perceived as being a national, no, an international disaster, an embarrassment to the nation. They were portrayed as traitors, hooligans and brawlers. A disgrace. They had been emotionally detached from the support of a country that was as confused as it was upset. But on October 1, 1972, after they had rallied with three consecutive victories in Moscow to capture the summit series 4-3-1 in games, all was forgiven. The prerogative of the fans had been exercised, and Team Canada was again the toast of the country, its members, stars and living legends. And the feeling has never died.

"When we got home I got off the plane and I kissed the ground, I was so happy to be back," said centre Phil Esposito, arguably the best player throughout the series, though his brilliance was overshadowed by the flare for the dramatic and heroics of Paul Henderson. "It was so good to be back home again. I'll never go back."

"It was probably the greatest flight coming home," said centre Marcel Dionne. "Guys just went crazy. You talk about mature people, but the pressure was finally off. I remember when we got back to Montreal, at the airport. I saw Trudeau, the prime minister, get into a fire truck with Peter Mahovlich and drive around the airport. Unbelievable."

A few seconds after Trudeau had welcomed home the team, and the first stirring, impromptu rendition of "O Canada" had been sung, defenceman Serge Savard grabbed an autographed hockey stick that assistant coach John Ferguson had carefully transported home from Moscow and presented it to the prime minister, right in front of a bemused and speechless Ferguson. But nothing mattered...

"I was on the float at the airport," explained Savard, "when I took Fergie's stick and gave it to the prime minister. Fergie never said a word. But the next day, the prime minister saw the story in the newspaper and he returned the stick."

In Montreal several players left the others to return home and resume their lives and careers. The bulk of Team Canada proceeded to Toronto, where they were caravaned by a 36-car motorcade, along highways and under overpasses draped with banners and cheering fans, to a thundering reception at Nathan Phillips Square, where they were greeted by an estimated 80,000 rain-soaked fans, all with swelled chests, all proudly singing the national anthem. It was a tearful and joyous love-in.

Seventeen years later, like a work of art, or a piece of music, the moment continues to play on in the memory of the players and the fans.

"I don't think any of us really comprehended what the series meant, what effect it had, until it was over," said Henderson, who scored the winning goal in the final three games and literally had become a living legend. "People still come up to me and shake my hand. And it probably affects me more today than it did back then. I talk about the goal at least 300 days a year. People haven't forgotten it, but then it certainly transcended being just a hockey series. It was more than just that.

"At first, I got sick of talking about it for a while, the first three or four months. There was absolutely no privacy. It got to be a bit of a pain. But I don't feel that way now. It's a special memory and I honestly can't think of anything better with which to be associated.

"You know, I really think the series is still changing me all these years later. When I came back, people were saying to me, well, you just wrote yourself into the Canadian history books and I would say, 'Get serious.' But that series gave me a profile I wouldn't have had otherwise, and I wouldn't still be known now.

Financially it was very rewarding, too. But in terms of being known, it put the finishing touches on that. The magnitude was so great.

"I can't believe the stories I hear, either. Even today. I remember one lady I was talking to recently. She told me about how she was moving and was unpacking some boxes the day of the final game. She was carrying two of her best plates, very expensive, when I scored the goal. Well, she got so excited she threw the plates into the air. She couldn't believe it. I've got a million stories like that, like the couple who said I saved their marriage. It's incredible. And I keep hearing new stories every time I travel. But I really believe that series touched a lot of people.

"For me, by going to Russia, you learned to appreciate what we have as Canadians. People want to talk about socialism and they cut up our country. Well, go over there and you'll realize what a great country we have. You learn to appreciate it. You hear all these minority groups going on all the time — well, I'd like to see them over there. We've got rights, and they've got the right to shut up about our country."

In a country where hockey is almost a religion, that series, besides salvaging pride and swelling chests, drew the country closer together, giving it a focus and a national unity that hadn't existed for decades. Perhaps not since the last war. There was, of course, tension between French and English, East and West, back then. But for twenty-seven days, while it never completely went away, the tension wasn't so acute. It was as if a truce had been called. There's plenty of time to fight after the hockey game....

Canadians from coast to coast had something precious to grasp, something that belonged to every one of them because it was in their hearts, something to raise their hopes, twist their emotions, and ultimately bring joy to their lives. There was not only a unique feeling of knowing what it was to be a Canadian on September 28, 1972, but an attendant pride in being one, too.

For this was a series that had all the components to hold the attention, and stir the emotions, from that shocking 7-3 opening-night defeat, to the struggle for vindication, to the feeling of betrayal and the ensuing loss of support, to the comeback that seemingly defied odds. It was dramatics of the tallest order.

"When I think back on it, I think what we did was a great accomplishment, no question," said winger J.P. Parise. "We faced tremendous odds throughout the whole thing. And after they had won the fifth game, all they needed was one point. *One point.* That series was the biggest thrill of my life. It gave me credibility in pursuing my career in the National Hockey League. I had two mediocre seasons before the series and I think I had my best overall season right after it. There's no question it made me stronger. It gave me all kinds of confidence. It showed a lot of people that you can play with the best. Sometimes when I go back and watch the NHL games now, I think, God, did I play at that level?"

"I don't think it was until the last day of the series that we really knew the impact the series would ultimately have and how important it had become then," said winger Ron Ellis. "Emotions were so high we really didn't realize the impact. We just wanted to fight back the best we could, and it took me, personally, a while to realize what we had done. When we left the country, after all, we weren't exactly loved, and I don't think we really knew how the people were reacting, except for the telegrams we were receiving over there in Moscow. But I think we got stronger as the series went on. If we had played another ten games, I don't know what would have happened, but I think we would've done well. We were really coming together as a team in those last couple of games."

It was a series that had profound effects on the lives of the players, but also drastically changed the face of a game that had been divided by political and idiosyncratic borders. The window of the world had been opened for a revealing exchange and the results were glorious. For almost two decades, the burning question of which country was superior on the ice had demanded an answer, and it was finally given, even if it wasn't entirely conclusive.

That the answer wasn't as obvious, either, as what many of us had expected, only enhanced the spectacle. The best Canada could muster − its paid professionals − were supposed to have throttled the Soviets, swept them in eight games, or so we thought. But instead, we received an invaluable lesson. If there was a hidden charm to the series, it was in the revelations and the changes that would follow.

The Soviets had proven themselves back then the masters of conditioning − physical and emotional. They were prepared in all areas. And at the time, the conditioning programs of NHL players were laughable, by Soviet standards in 1972 and by NHL standards today. But they have changed. On the ice, there was also a great exchange of ideas and systems as a result, the best of two very different styles of play dissected, reviewed, reworked and adopted. Our minor hockey systems were revamped, the accent placed heavily on player development and improved coaching methods. We hadn't been proven wrong in our intent or direction, nor were we proven inferior, but we had simply been privy to another approach, shown there was vast room for improvement. Perhaps the greatest aspect of the series then, is that none of the revelations went unheeded. Changes were made.

"That series was almost our lifestyle against theirs, communism versus capitalism," said Clarke. "I think what it did was make us realize how good the European players were. Even those games we played in Sweden and Czechoslovakia were tough games. All of sudden in that series we're saying to ourselves, 'Goddamn it, these guys are playing as well as us.' It wasn't an easy thing to admit at the time, either, because everyone thought the NHL was the best and that was it."

Fifteen years later, at the 1987 Canada Cup, the level of play in terms of pure skill was undoubtedly better than the 1972 series, but the difference between the Soviets and Team Canada was still small. In a thrilling three-game final, the Canadians won 2-1, all three games ending with 6-5 scores — coincidentally the very same score as game eight in 1972 — and the final goal arrived with just 1:26 remaining in the third game.

"The whole '72 series was interesting," said coach Harry Sinden. "I'm not so sure, though, whether Soviet hockey has benefitted as much as we have. I really haven't seen a great improvement in their teams since 1972, but I have to think we could put together a stronger team now than we had, but I don't think the Soviets' team would be that much different.

"Soviet hockey has been evolving a certain way since I first played them in 1957 with the Whitby Dunlops. But their fundamental basic belief remains unchanged. It's the tremendous emphasis on getting into better physical condition than anyone they play, in any sport.

"In skating ability, they have an edge over North American teams. Their balance and agility are superior to ours. There's a distinct Soviet skating style — shorter, choppier strides.

"That shorter stride is responsible for the better balance. It's easier to have lateral movement and it may be the reason why they read the play quicker. They don't stop skating when they take a pass or shoot, the way our guys do. They accelerate as the puck comes to them and they can pick it up without changing strides.

"They do slap the puck more now and simply shoot it more than they used to. They used to get to the blue line, and if there was no play to be made, they would retreat, regroup and come up with another rush. They're doing less of that now. The shots used to come from the slot, too, but now they do more shooting off the wings. They've learned to work the boards and corners so well now they're tough to handle. But in terms of teams, I think we would have a stronger team than them."

"Because of that series," added Parise, "hockey right now is a lot better. No question. There are better skaters, the players are a little bigger perhaps, but it helped us expand our game with different strategies."

"I think the series, the whole experience, has been good for us," said Tony Esposito, who had been reluctant to participate. "It has made us better for it. It was a wonderful thing. The thing I remember most is how we underestimated them, but who could blame us? The so-called hockey experts, the bigwigs in the NHL, kept telling us we were so far superior. It was certainly a learning experience. A great experience."

There is, however, a wide divergence of views as to which country profitted the most from the exchange, if it can be truly measured. And seventeen years later, the memories are not only fresh, but a degree of disenchantment remains, too, with the series, and the Soviets.

"I think the Russians learned more from us," said Gilbert. "They learned more about bodychecking. And to improvise. Against us they were just robots. They had the same expression, whether they scored or we scored. That pissed me off, too. I felt like saying, 'Look you idiots, show some expression.' I was pissed off. And when you bodychecked them, they would just continue on. Show some emotion, guys!

"I didn't respect them, which translated into, 'How the fuck can you live in this country?' They had the same expressions on their faces all the time. That's not my idea of a good team."

"The biggest changes that came from the series were to the game," said goalie Eddie Johnston. "We ultimately learned some things about their game and adapted to the Russian style, and they did the same from us. We've both taken the best of both games and tried to incorporate them."

"I think it changed the NHL," said winger Dennis Hull. "Usually it's an individual who causes the change. No one slapped the puck like Bobby Hull until he came along, and then suddenly all these kids are coming up who can shoot the puck 100 miles per hour because they all started emulating Bobby Hull.

"Then there was Bobby Orr. A defenceman didn't dare take off to score goals. Four or five goals a year was considered great. But now, if a defenceman doesn't score 15, 20 goals, what is he?

"The Russians showed us a different way to play. The way

they skated and handled the puck — they were absolutely great puck handlers — and now look at the way kids handle the puck."

"I think what the series has done more than anything else is create an elite system in (minor) hockey," said defenceman Pat Stapleton, who since retiring has been heavily involved in instructional clinics and camps for both coaches and players at the amateur level. "The majority of dollars go to the elite clubs, the travelling clubs, not to the masses. I think there should be more going to the masses than to the elite.

"In our game today, there are more and more travelling teams (considered the top minor-hockey teams). So the kids, if they're not on a travelling team by the time they're thirteen or fourteen, they start to look to other sports. It's chasing the kids out of hockey.

"I think a lot of parents are trying to live their dreams through their kids. They want them to make it in the NHL. But there's more to it than that. There's a lot more to be learned from playing team sports — important life skills, such as working together, achieving a common goal, and physical fitness.

"Now, if a kid isn't elite, he feels like a failure. So he gets out of hockey, but then you'll find they're coming back at age thirty just because they like to play. Hockey was my goal, not my parents'. I lived near a rink that was only five or six blocks away, so I would get up in the morning and ride my bike to the rink. I did it because I wanted to play, not because my parents wanted me to grow up and play in the NHL."

Still, there has been considerable progress at the minor level, and in the NHL. While there was much reluctance to adapt — we had won, after all — any successful team these days has no fewer than two assistant coaches, a physiotherapist, conditioning programs, and it works heavily on strategy and preparation.

"I think it really helped our hockey," offered assistant coach John Ferguson, who later became general manager of the New York Rangers, then Winnipeg Jets, and in April, 1989, managed Team Canada in the world championships in Stockholm. "We've taken goaltending training methods, for instance, and conditioning methods from them. I think that gave rise to year-round conditioning. I mean, they were in such great shape in that series. When I was a general manager, I hired strength coaches and used diet programs, and put a lot of players on weight programs and things. It made us realize how important conditioning is."

"It was just great practising with our guys," said defenceman Joceyln Guevremont, who in the '72 series departed the team prior to game five. "I got to learn. I saw Russia. If I had to do it again, I would. I think the series is helping guys today. It's helping increase the players' pension plan. And it was great hockey, great for the game."

"The Soviets were more flexible, the Canadians more physical," said Soviet centre Boris Mikhailov. "But we have since combined the best qualities of both styles. It was an exchange of styles and both teams have learned."

"I think Wayne Gretzky would have been Wayne Gretzky if Canada had never played the Russians," countered winger Wayne Cashman. "He doesn't play a Russian style of hockey. In that series, the Russians had had more time to practise. The nucleus of Team Canada was a very talented team, but our conditioning was off. Eventually, though, superior talent and determination won. The Russian system doesn't reach out for pride, either. We reached back and won that series."

"Maybe that's the one thing they don't have," agreed Sinden. "They don't have the mental conditioning, the mental toughness that our guys have."

Emotion was obviously a definite factor in the series, the Canadians' resolve, pride and determination showing through especially in the final three games. They played with heart, occasionally got too wound up and got carried away, but were nevertheless driven to succeed. Pride soon was measured in defiance and victories. Before it was over, they reaffirmed their integrity and character in an incomparable show. Of course, part of the pride wasn't simply born of trailing the Soviets, but also of the public reaction in Canada to their losing.

Whatever, when the series was over, it had affected different players in many different ways. Some were inspired to reach for greater heights of excellence in the upcoming season, in their careers. Some, though, experienced a huge letdown when they returned home. They had ridden an emotional roller-coaster and the ride was over, the fanfare soon died and the games didn't have the same importance or intensity. Depression settled in. And some were simply so drained by it all, it literally took months to recover. But all were indelibly touched by the series, even the likes of Cashman, whose disregard for playing the Russians hasn't wavered. Like big Phil Esposito, for whom he now works in New York, they had been conscripted to serve their country and they had obeyed.

"Well, it wasn't exactly something I had dreamed about as a kid or anything," said Cashman. "When I was growing up, you dreamt about winning the Stanley Cup, and I don't think that series could compare to that. What it boils right down to is it was a great experience, but it wasn't something I had thought about for a long time. I didn't dream about it because I had never considered it ever happening. It was something I did and I enjoyed it."

"Ask anyone what they were doing and they remember," said Savard. "I've won a lot of Stanley Cups, but that still has to rate as the biggest thrill."

"I think all the series played now, the Canada Cup, et cetera, are judged by that 1972 series," said defenceman Don Awrey. "Every time Canada plays against the Russians, we're favoured to win, even though in '72 we had to struggle to come back. In the Canada Cup, the ball is always in our court. We've got the home ice, the home fans, the food is ours. If it was the Sweden Cup, and we had to go over there, our chances of winning would be less. We had a lot to overcome playing over in Russia, and that just adds to the accomplishment."

"It was amazing," said defenceman Bobby Orr, whose injured knee prevented him from playing in 1972. "I went on the trip anyway and I couldn't believe it. To go over there, down by a game, then lose the next one and need to win three in a row.... It was amazing, especially when you consider the conditions and the circumstances and everything.

"What that team did, well, it was just one helluva team. I don't think anyone realized when Espo made that speech in Vancouver just how powerful it was. He brought the team together; that was the rallying cry. The team went to Sweden for ten days and started believing in themselves. I can still remember that series like it was yesterday."

"This series helped me immensely," said Bobby Clarke. "Some of the top NHL players it didn't help as much because they were already at the top of their game, but for guys like Henderson and Ellis and myself it helped our careers. People started to take notice.

"For me, I've always felt that the first Stanley Cup we won was the biggest thing I won. When you're a kid, growing up, you dream of carrying it around the ice, and when you play for years and then finally win it, it's something special. But this series was incredibly emotional and everything fell into place so quickly."

"Once it was over, that's when you enjoyed the series," said defenceman Brad Park. "It was so intense. And criss-crossing the country when we were supposed to romp and we weren't romping, it was a little difficult to enjoy.

"But it's a great memory. Something to reminisce about and use as a starting point for NHL-Soviet hockey. It does have its place in history and I think it would've had whether we had won or not. I still think about the series every once in a while, too. It's not something you dwell on every day because you've got other things to do, but you think about the players you played with, and all that hype at the time. Yeah, it's a special memory."

"When it was over," added Sinden, "it was such an emotional experience. Everyone was just exhausted. It was tough to handle, an incredible moment for hockey and the players."

"I don't think it really changed my life, but I'm glad for the opportunity and very proud to have taken part," said winger Yvon Cournoyer. "Our names will be remembered for that series forever. I won ten Stanley Cups with the Montreal Canadiens and each one was special, each one had a different feeling. But this was special, too, and it had a different feeling.

"It was a good experience in my life, to represent your country, to play in the first series, and it became bigger and bigger as it went on and even after it was over. In terms of experience, it was the best I had. Ever. It became country versus country and you don't have that too often."

"To the Russians," said Parise, "the whole thing about the series was what great public relations it was for the communist regime. The hockey was secondary. Even our own press was against us, which probably made it easier for the Russians."

"I guess the good guys won another one, though," offered centre Peter Mahovlich. "That's the way it is, the good guys and the bad guys. We had the white hats, they had the red hats, I guess. But it was politics. It was more than just hockey.

"Like I said, if you were to write a Hollywood script like that, people would say what a bunch of crap. But it was certainly a bonus in my career. I've played on four Stanley Cup winning teams, but nothing compared to that series. The first Stanley Cup was great. The second, too, the same with the third and fourth. And I played on some great teams, that Montreal team that only lost eight games one season.

"But nothing compared to that goal I scored in the second game of the series, or just participating in Team Canada. When I look at it now, at that time in my career, I didn't deserve to be there, but I went there with thirty-five other guys and went there to play, to work hard. It all paid off and turned out pretty well.

"When it was over, we just came home and won the Stanley Cup," said winger Frank Mahovlich, his brother's teammate with the Canadiens back then. "So I don't think it affected me too much. It's nice to see places like Russia once. Yes, it was a special series, their best against our best. What can you say?"

* * *

Interestingly, the impact and lasting effects of the series had as much social implications as sporting. There was now, for the players, a better appreciation for Canada, and an improved regard for the Soviets. These players had been the first to cross those borders, via that format.

"I remember exchanging gifts before one of the games," said Hull. "I got one of those dolls that comes apart and has another doll inside. I also got a model of the tower in Red Square. They're great memories. For me, it was the highlight of my hockey career. You know, it was the first time the NHL ever played the Russians. Anyone you talk to over twenty-five years old remembers where they were when we won it. It was very exciting.

"I guess I felt relief, really, when we finally did win it. We were supposed to win — that's what all the scouts had said. We were representing Canada and the league and then to be humiliated if we lost… I think we proved for a little while that our hockey system was the best one.

"We all enjoyed the competition. We knew this wasn't the NHL. You weren't playing Oakland or Vancouver, so everyone was giving a hundred percent. The level of play was more elevated than normal. The next season, I had one of my best years. We were six weeks ahead in conditioning."

"But some guys," said Johnston, "never got it back again until

Christmas. It took a long time for some guys to recover. It was emotionally draining. At the very beginning, I don't think any of us really knew what we were getting into. But as the series progressed, we sure did. And we knew we were making history. We just hoped it would be the right kind.

"The one thing we all learned when it was over was to appreciate what we had in Canada. There was no comparison between the two countries, and it took a trip over there and those games to drive the point home. You know, for more than just the players I think the point was made.

"It turned out to be more than just a hockey series, too, more than just two teams playing a game. A lot of pride came into play — pride in yourself, pride in your team, pride in your country. It was two hockey teams, but it was also two countries playing.

"I still think about the series a lot. It's the sort of thing that happens to you once in a lifetime and you never forget it. Now when the Russian teams come over, or I see the old posters — I've got one on the wall at home — you realize just what went on.

"This series was the first, the first time our best met their best, and that kind of makes it a little more special. When it was over, well, I'd never seen guys crying and hugging like that. It was excitement and relief. Country versus country, it was that, but we called it war."

"As a part of Canada's history, I think it would have been forgotten quickly if we had lost," said centre Jean Ratelle. "It's just like the Russians probably tried to forget about it. It was the first series, and I know people stopped doing things to watch, and didn't go to work so they could catch the game, so in that sense, it was a pretty important part of our history.

"It's hard to say exactly how I felt at the time, whether I knew how significant a part of our history it would become. I think I approached it as any other important series in the league. You know you have to do well, but you don't let it occupy you all the time. I think that's how I approached it.

"I think the series was more than just Canada-Russia, though. It was worldwide, it seemed. Anytime you arrange nations to play, it's good politically. It was good for everyone. You play a sport and may the best team wins. But I think you always maintain a mutual respect between the Russians and us.

"I don't know if I have a fondest memory. There's nothing really special that sticks out for me personally. I think what's special is that we played, and that we won. I think that series was the best experience in my career. I never won the Stanley Cup, so the series is kind of special. I think it was important to the fans, too. I mean, there's no doubt Canada got caught up in it, but the fans just want their team to win. The fans are doing their part by cheering for somebody."

"It was the best experience, the most difficult of my career," added Gilbert. "There was so much pressure. I think the whole thing was overcoming the way we did, from being so far behind. Having to really pull back, and study hockey at a different forum. We really had to study them, too, dig down deep, and think, 'What could work against them?' But winning it, coming from behind, is the biggest reward."

Seventeen years later, neither the significance nor the memories have faded. Life goes on, but a special chapter in history continues to touch those who were a part of it, who lived it, and even those who watched. To some, the memories are the fondest;

to some their remains a scuffed edge. But again it seems more of an anti-Soviet sentiment, a realization provided by hindsight of what an immense task they had undertaken with insufficient preparation.

"I had scored seventy-six goals the season before and at that time everyone said it was because of Bobby Orr," said Phil Esposito. "I knew I had talent. Other people started realizing it after that series.

"But I still think the series is something we should never have done, none of that should have happened. Not at all. We had nothing to gain and everything to lose. I didn't want to play, but I had no choice."

"That series changed our way of thinking," said Dionne. "It opened up our eyes to another way of playing and preparing. I think it had the most effect on us working on our skills. Looking back, when you retire, you talk about the things that don't come around too often. We saw Russia, the whole system, the whole scenario we didn't understand fully. It was a real eye opener."

There were also concerns among some NHL owners, the ones who believed the series shouldn't have been played. Theirs was not a fear of having their players proven inferior though, but of losing stars through injury, and having players from several different NHL teams playing together for a month. They wondered, accurately enough, if they would have the same feeling when they returned.

"There's no question that series is a big part of Canada's history, but one thing I still remember is the rivalries," said Park. "The Rangers and Bruins used to have one of the biggest rivalries in the NHL, and it was never the same after that series. Because you had played with the guys, you didn't have the same hatred after that. It used to be pure hatred. But it was never the same."

"That was the owners' concern," said Hull. "Over the years, one of the things you didn't do was talk to the opposition. You weren't playing against friends. But with Team Canada, you get to know people over a two-month period, and the intensity in some rivalries wasn't there anymore. Now, I know guys like Savard, Cournoyer, Lapointe, that I didn't know before."

The shortcomings, though, paled in the spotlight of adulation that grew when the series was completed. The owners could never have devised a promotion for their players and their league that reached the heights the series gave it. Too much good came out of that series, especially for the competitors. And the benefits drifted far from just the NHL. They ultimately affected a country.

"Everywhere we went, there was an ovation, a celebration. People appreciated what the team did, the way it played, the obstacles it overcame, and the way it won," said Johnston. "And people finally realized that maybe the booing and the criticisms earlier in the series were unfounded. It was a series that was tough emotionally on everyone.

"It's a series I don't think anyone will forget. Oh, they may forget the odd detail, but everyone remembers thirty-four seconds left and Paul Henderson scoring. It's a series, a collection of great moments, that changed his life. He became a legend after that. To this day, he's not remembered for being a Maple Leaf, he's remembered for the goals — maybe the goal — he scored for Canada."

"It sure had a big effect on my life," said Sinden. "Out of that series came the general manager's job in Boston, and I've had that job ever since.

"The dramatic ending was amazing, that a team didn't lose in a strange land, on a strange ice rink. That made it the greatest possible, to comeback in those conditions.

"I was happy just to be involved. The business I was working for had gone bankrupt when the team was being formed, so I had nothing to do. I've talked to the players since then, too, and they can recite what happened in that series — it's indelible in their minds. Winning the Stanley Cup is great, but others have won it. No one else has done what we did then or since. I told the players that, too.

"Everyone just got caught up in what was going on. It was a memorable series, but I can't think of a series or a team that captured the attention of a country the way this team did. Maybe in the World Cup of soccer it happens, especially in the Latin countries, but never in hockey.

"It's interesting, too, that we were even called Team Canada. We coined that name in 1972, and it has stuck ever since for all tournaments. Even other countries use it. I remember there was a big debate over the name, but out of it all we needed a name that was easily written in French and English. It did seem weird at first, but it really caught on. It's just another of the many memories.

"You know, I can honestly say I loved every moment of that series. It's something no one can take away from us, either. We were treading dangerous waters, we were close to losing, but if that job hadn't come along I'd still be looking to start up that bankrupt company."

The series has had profound effects on the hockey world —

financially and in terms of exposure. It made hockey big time, truly a world sport, leading to Canada Cup series in 1976, 1981, 1984 and 1987. There was also a summit in 1974 with the World Hockey Association, and the NHL has twice played its All-Stars against the Soviets — in 1979 and 1987. On top of all that, there have been Soviet club tours through the NHL, and the exchanges have carried over into junior and amateur hockey, as well. Beyond that, professionals are now welcome in the Olympics and the world championship has become a much more significant tournament.

The most recent development was the release of four top Soviet players — Viatcheslav Fetisov, Sergei Makarov, Igor Larionov and Sergei Priakhin — to play in the NHL in the 1989-90 season.

"None of us could foresee what effects that series would have," said Eagleson. "We had no idea it would become the big business it has become. But the big lesson from the series was that there was a helluva lot of good hockey being played around the world.

"In Canada, it was the greatest thing for our generation. That series created a flow of warmth and happiness across the country that hasn't been matched. Even to this day I cannot buy a beer in Montreal, because if I walk into a bistro in Montreal, everyone remembers me from the series. It's amazing.

"I remember in December of 1972, after we had gotten back, there was an air strike and I was stuck at the train station in Montreal. Aggie and I had six hours to kill. All of a sudden, there's this huge crowd around us, everyone talking about the series and all of it in French.

"If we had lost, well, it would've been depressing. I mean, just losing the first game was depressing enough. But of the sixty-odd goals scored in the series, I bet I can remember seventy-five percent of them for both teams.

"My favourite story about coming back, though, is about a letter I saw from Wilder Penfield criticizing our team. We got cut to ratshit, saying this was the worst thing to happen to Canada-Soviet relations. Then I got a letter from Ambassador Ford. It said, 'Dear Mr. Eagleson, I read the reports in Canada saying this series had bad effects on relations between the two countries, but there are 200 million Russians who saw our hockey and it is one of the most beneficial things to our relations.'

"When we got back, I decided to take the family out of town to Upper Canada Village to relax. It was a dreary weekend, but it was comfortable and casual. The clincher came after reading all those things in the newspapers. People are saying Team Ugly led by a diplomatic disaster. I always said I can accept criticism from people if they were there. So I'm wondering did it affect public opinion that way and did we waste nine months of our time? And I was still tired.

"I went into this plaza in Cornwall, a lunch counter, and it was just the four of us, my wife and two kids, sitting there, and I can see these kids across the way. The one kid had this bright, shocking red hair. I'll never forget it. The kid kept looking at me, and finally he comes over and says, 'Are you the guy from Team Canada?' I said yes and he yelled across the restaurant, 'Hey, guys, this is Mr. Eagleson!' Next thing you know, they're all over, standing around me, asking questions about the series. That burst the balloon of pessimism for me. I was going to quit the NHL Players' Association if the reaction was that we were going to get carved.

"The special feeling still exists among that group we had over there, too. We called it Team 50, the players, coaches, trainers, doctors. It's the best thing that ever happened to all of us. And it was a great thing for all Canadians."

As journalist Dick Beddoes put it, Napoleon didn't take Moscow, the Nazis got within twenty-one miles in 1943, but in a war of a different kind, Team Canada conquered Moscow.

"You can't write hockey history without writing about that series and Paul Henderson's goal," he said. "In Canadian history, we had the FLQ crisis in 1970, the taking of Vimy Ridge in 1917, and we had VE Day in 1945. VE Day and the celebration in 1972 were the biggest this country has had.

"This is our national sport. To have won the first one at the summit, thirty-four seconds left, has to rank as the premier hockey happening in Canadian history. You can't write about Canada without writing about that series.

"I've always said, hockey is war under wraps. The series reflected our hockey culture. We did misbehave. We were what we are and we won because of something somehow Canadian to do what you have to do to win. We're not gentlemanly in our national sport. Ben Johnson was a big thing for a while, but everybody in every small town plays hockey. For twenty-seven sustained days, all the attendant things, it was the best. The players were made demigods. Of anything I covered, this was it because of the historic nature of pros playing against pros for the first time."

"It was a moment and moments are easier to remember than periods of time," said Ken Dryden. "It's one of the few to which we apply another memory, remembering where we were at the time. But I haven't run into anyone who has said it wasn't the most vivid of memories.

"What was almost the biggest charge for me, watching again, was the great sense of distance...the voices of Foster Hewitt and Brian Conacher...it was almost the foreign-correspondent voice, coming down the pipe one hundred miles away. It had that same crackly, distorted quality as the Second World War voices of a Walter Cronkite or an Edward R. Murrow. That was the sound. And the other thing was the sound of the Canadian fans. They were just remarkable. I got more chills hearing those fans again — it brought back many memories."

And finally...

"When I look back personally, it was probably my greatest accomplishment, playing with that team," said Parise. "Here I am, a little guy from Smooth Rock Falls, and I'm playing on a line with Phil Esposito, the best forward in the NHL.

"My dad was responsible for my playing hockey. He left me on my own. He didn't push me or anything. But he made me a little rink, you know. When I scored my first goal in Winnipeg, people told me later that my dad had big tears in his eyes. You know, here was his son participating in such a series, representing his country.

"When I think back about that series, what I visualize most is how I had made my dad proud. Afterwards, when I got home, my hometown gave me a day. It was well-planned. They had this big sign that said Home of J.P. Parise. The mayor declared a holiday in Smooth Rock Falls. Yeah, I have some pretty fine memories from that series."

The days Canada stood still.

KAMIN & HOWELL INC.
is one of the world's leading packagers
and publishers of books.
They have produced more than 70 titles.